NEW YORK STATE
GRADE 4
ELEMENTARY-LEVEL
ENGLISH LANGUAGE
ARTS TEST

2nd EDITION

DEBORA S. WHITING
DONNA C. OLIVERIO

BARRON'S

Dedication

To DJW, ASW, BJW, AND EGW with love. Thank you for belieiving in me.
To all my students with gratitude. Thank you for being the best teachers.

DSW

All inquiries should be addressed to:
Barron's Educational Series, Inc.
250 Wireless Boulevard
Hauppauge, New York 11788
www.barronseduc.com

ISBN-13: 978-0-7641-3862-1
ISBN-10: 0-7641-3862-6

International Standard Serial No.: 1937-092X

Printed in the United States of America

9 8 7 6 5 4 3

Contents

ACKNOWLEDGMENTS

A Universe of Thanks to:

- all the children and their families, who have enriched my life throughout the years

- the wonderful students at Sag Harbor and Riverhead Public Schools

- my colleagues and administrators at Sag Harbor

- my loving family and friends

Donna Christina

INTRODUCTION FOR STUDENTS

It was late January. Everyone at Moosehead Elementary School was wondering why the students in Mr. Antler's fourth-grade class were celebrating. After all, this was around the time that fourth graders would be taking the important test with the long name: The New York State English Language Arts (ELA) Assessment. The name alone is enough to get you nervous or make you want to snooze.

Why, then, did the children in Mr. Antler's class look so cheerful and relaxed? Like you, they have been preparing for the ELA test ever since they first entered school many years ago. They have been listening to their teacher and practicing their language arts skills, so they're actually looking forward to the test. And, so can you! By following your teacher's instructions and doing the practice exercises in this book, you will be able to show everyone, especially yourself, how well you are able to read, write, listen, and think. So, like the students in Mr. Antler's class, get ready to celebrate the test!

The ELA is given over a three-day period. Each day is outlined below.

Day 1: 4–5 reading selections, 28 multiple-choice questions, 45 minutes

Day 2: Part 1—Listen to a passage read aloud, write 2 short answers and 1 long response, 45 minutes

Day 3: Read 2 selections, write 3 short responses and 1 long response, 60 minutes

We hope you enjoy the interesting stories and activities in this book. They were written to help you improve your language arts skills and to help you become familiar with the types of questions asked on the ELA test.

Think of yourselves as the eager students in Mr. Antler's class. With practice and a positive attitude, you can rise to the challenge and celebrate the ELA test!

In this review book, you will find

- a separate chapter for each section of the ELA test
- three complete practice tests, along with detailed answers
- appendices at the back of the book, which give you a summary of important information

SYMBOLS AND GRAPHICS

The symbols and graphics shown below are used throughout the book to help guide your learning.

TIME MANAGEMENT TIPS

The ELA exam is a timed test. You must plan your time so that you are able to finish the test. Don't worry: Most students are able to finish the test within the time allowed. Look for the clock symbol to give you tips on managing your time.

KNOW THE TASK

Learn about each section of the ELA.

TAKE A CLOSER LOOK

Understanding the questions and what is expected is very important. Learn how questions can be broken down to understand them better.

TIPS TO KEEP YOU ON TARGET

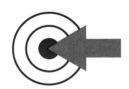

Tips are given throughout the book to help you understand what it takes to be successful.

GET READY TO LISTEN

This is a reminder that you need to do certain things to be ready to listen effectively.

CHECK YOUR WORK

This symbol lets you know that you must look over your work and check it carefully.

OVERVIEW FOR FAMILIES AND TEACHERS

FREQUENTLY ASKED QUESTIONS ABOUT THE ELA

The chart below gives you an overview of the exam.

WHAT ARE THE DIFFERENT SECTIONS OF THE ELA TEST?

The chart below outlines each day and section of the test.

New York State English Language Arts Test		
Day 1	Day 2	Day 3
Session 1 45 minutes Multiple-Choice Section ■ Read 4–5 selections. ■ Answer 28 questions.	Session 2 45 minutes Listening Section ■ 2 short answers ■ 1 long response	Session 3 60 minutes Reading and Writing ■ Read 2 selections. ■ Write 3 short answers, 1–2 on each of the selections read. ■ Write 1 long response based on both reading selections.

WHAT SKILLS ARE NEEDED TO BE SUCCESSFUL ON THE FOURTH-GRADE ELA EXAM?

Day 1—Reading Comprehension Section

- Read for main idea and details.
- Remember information from reading.
- Quickly reread to locate information to help answer questions.
- Think about information, draw conclusions, and make predictions.

Day 2—Listening Section Skills

- Remember information you hear.
- Take notes and organize information.
- Write answers to question using information from the listening selection.

Day 3—Reading and Response Writing Skills

- Read 2 selections and write a response(s) related to each.
- Write a response that includes details from both reading selections.

WHEN IS THE FOURTH-GRADE ELA GIVEN?

The assessment is scheduled in the winter of fourth grade (early January), depending on state guidelines and your school district calendar. Please check with your child's teacher for exact dates and times.

HOW IS THE ELA SCORED?

To help ensure that all students across the state are graded uniformly, the New York State Education Department provides scorers (teachers) with rubrics (scoring guides) and scored sample answers. See Chapter 4 (pages 96–99 and 110–111) for examples of rubrics, which will give you an idea of how student work is to be assessed.

HOW IS THE ELA DIFFERENT FROM OTHER TESTS?

- Every student in New York State will take the exam.
- The test is timed.
- The tests are scored by a group of teachers using state guidelines.

WHAT TESTING MODIFICATIONS ARE AVAILABLE FOR STUDENTS WITH SPECIAL NEEDS?

Testing accommodations are being reviewed by the New York State Education Department. Modifications such as having directions read aloud may be indicated on a student's Individualized Education Program (IEP) or 504 plan and approved by the Committee on Special Education (CSE). If your child has an IEP, you should check with his teacher or Special Education Director for information regarding eligibility for testing accommodations.

WHEN WILL I KNOW MY CHILD'S ELA SCORE?

The scores are usually released to school districts in late summer. Districts then send students' individual scores to parents.

WHAT DO THE SCORES MEAN?

- Scores on the assessment range from 1 to 4.
- A score of 4 indicates that the student's performance on the assessment exceeds state standards.
- A score of 3 indicates that the student's work meets state standards.
- A score of either 1 or 2 is below state standards. A score of 2 might mean that your child is struggling in one or more areas and may require some extra support. A score of 1 indicates that your child's work is below the standards set for fourth-grade students in New York State. Additional instruction and intervention services will be needed to reach standards.

WILL MY CHILD BE HELD BACK IN FOURTH GRADE IF SHE RECEIVES A LOW SCORE?

The ELA assessment alone should not determine whether your child is retained in fourth grade. Classroom performance and other factors play an important role in the decision to promote or retain a child.

WHAT CAN A PARENT/GUARDIAN DO TO HELP A CHILD PREPARE FOR THE ELA ASSESSMENT?

The learning process is triangular in nature: Research shows that student achievement is greatly improved when the student, teacher, and parent/guardian work together. Although we strongly believe that the practice exercises in this review book will enhance student performance on the assessment, no single resource could ever replace the cumulative learning experiences that have shaped your child.

Please check with your child's teacher to see if there are any special instructions regarding testing procedures. Be sure your child has a good night's sleep on the nights before the assessment, and a healthy breakfast on the mornings of the exam. If your child appears nervous, explain to him that most people experience some degree of test anxiety. Try to be as reassuring and positive as possible. Send your child off to school with a message to simply do his best.

TO THE PARENT OR GUARDIAN

In fourth grade, your child will take the New York State English Language Arts (ELA) Assessment. The test is designed to measure how well students can read, write, listen, and think.

Barron's New York State Grade 4 English Language Arts Test contains exercises that mirror tasks students are expected to perform on the actual ELA assessment. It familiarizes children with test format and the different types of questions asked, thereby helping to improve student levels of confidence. When combined with an overall effective education program, this review book is likely to enhance student performance on the test.

Research has repeatedly shown that parental involvement is crucial to student success. There are several things you can do to improve children's language and literacy experiences:

1. Encourage your child to read a wide variety of material daily, such as books, magazines, and newspapers. Set aside time each day to read with her, and make it a pleasurable experience for both of you. Discuss story elements such as title, setting, characters, conflict, and resolution.
2. Make frequent, regular visits to the library. Bring home plenty of books for both you and your child. Encourage children to select reading material that interests them. Volunteer to read aloud to children material that is too difficult for them to read on their own. Ask the librarian and/or your child's teacher about book clubs, which give children an opportunity to share and discuss literature.

3. Promote good conversational and listening skills. Have frequent discussions with children about their studies. Play imaginative reading and vocabulary word games with synonyms/antonyms, facts/opinions, sight vocabulary, adjectives, and so forth. Emphasize to children the importance of paying attention when you or others speak to them.

4. Monitor the amount of time that children spend watching television or playing computer/video games. Discuss story elements after watching an age-appropriate movie or show together. Note the types of television programs your child likes to view and try to find reading material that reflects her television interests. Help your child understand the difference between fantasy and fact on television.

5. Promote a positive attitude toward written expression. Write notes to children at home, or send them off to school with a note from you in their lunch boxes. Encourage children to keep a journal, correspond with a pen pal, write a letter to the author of a favorite book, and write thank-you notes for gifts.

6. Provide a quiet place in the home for children to complete assignments. Emphasize the importance of homework completion. To improve children's spelling and vocabulary abilities, keep a child-friendly dictionary and thesaurus on hand.

7. Be patient. The growing and learning process take time. Praise children as they acquire new literacy skills. Don't compare your child with others, but respect him as a special individual.

8. Overall, your behavior and attitude should convey to children that you value literacy and learning in general. Aim to create an environment that is rich in both print and the spoken word. When children see you reading and writing daily for meaningful purposes, they begin to understand the connection between their schoolwork and real life. They are then more likely to put forth greater effort into their studies.

TO THE TEACHER

We know firsthand the various challenges inherent in teaching fourth grade. It certainly seems as though much of the year is spent teaching difficult content information and preparing students for the rigorous state assessments. At times, our creativity feels stifled and we may even question our role as caring, effective educators.

This resource is designed to reflect current educational practices in language arts classrooms and to improve student performance on the ELA. By emphasizing effective language arts strategies, we believe we can provide students with appropriate, quality instruction while simultaneously preparing them for the test. Because the last thing we want to do is increase your workload, extra time and emphasis have been placed on scaffolding students' learning and providing responses with detailed explanations. Our goal is to make the ELA experience and language arts learning a positive one.

Each section of the ELA is represented by its own chapter in this review book. The reading selections are educational, engaging, and varied—including such topics as the environment, the Statue of Liberty, teddy bears, animals, and the history of roller coasters.

The Student Checklist at the end of Chapter 4 uses a graphic organizer to simplify the rubric concept. The Appendix contains two examples of more detailed rubrics, which are offered as samples and guides.

We believe your students will enjoy and learn from the original, rubric poem in Chapter 3. You may want to enlarge the poem for classroom display.

The Appendix is packed full of useful information. It contains an extensive list of important terms (e.g., fact/opinion, main idea, literary elements, transition words), complete with student-friendly definitions and examples. These words comprise the language and concepts of the ELA and of fourth grade in general; they are used in context throughout this resource. The Appendix also contains, among other items, an overview of the various genres, including strategies for understanding the different types of literary forms.

We know that you'll continue to do your best, and we wish you and your students all the best as you guide them through this milestone year in their lives.

READING/MULTIPLE CHOICE

OVERVIEW: SESSION 1

The shaded column of the chart below shows what you will be asked to do on Day 1.

New York State English Language Arts Test		
Day 1	Day 2	Day 3

Session 1
45 minutes
 	
Multiple-Choice Section
■ Read 4–5 selections.
■ Answer 28 questions.
	Session 2
	45 minutes
	
	Listening Section
	■ 2 short answers
	■ 1 long response
		Session 3
		60 minutes
		
		Reading and Writing
		■ Read 2 selections.
		■ Write 3 short answers,
		  1–2 on each of the
		  selections read.
		■ Write 1 long response
		  based on both reading
		  selections.

TIPS ON ANSWERING MULTIPLE-CHOICE QUESTIONS

- Read the question very carefully.
- Look back in the selection to find information that may help you answer the question.
- Read *all* answer choices, even if the first answer choice seems correct. Many questions have 2, 3, or 4 answers that may seem correct. You must always choose the BEST answer.
- Eliminate answer choices you know are wrong.
- Choose the best answer from the remaining choices, or make a good guess.
- Be very careful about skipping questions that you are unsure of. If you decide to skip a question and return to it later, you *must* remember to skip the matching number on your answer sheet.

TYPES OF QUESTIONS ASKED

There are different types of questions asked in the multiple-choice section of the assessment. Below you will find examples of the types of questions asked, followed by a list of what the questions expect you to be able to do.

Literal Comprehension Questions

- Recall or locate information from the selection.
- Understand information from the reading/listening selection.

Thinking and/or Reasoning Questions

- Think about the author's purpose.
- Identify the main idea of a selection.
- Make predictions.
- Compare and contrast.
- Use figurative language to understand text.
- Draw inferences and conclusions.

Vocabulary Questions

■ Use vocabulary strategies, such as determining the meaning of words from their context in the selection.

Note: Remember that some words have more than one meaning. Read the sentence containing the vocabulary word and the surrounding sentences for clues to the word's meaning in the selection. Pay attention to hints or clues that may be given in the details of a selection.

GUIDED PRACTICE

The guided practice section of this review book contains five selections. You will not be timed during the guided practice.

Directions: Read this poem about the wind. Then answer questions 1 through 6.

Wind Song

Anonymous

Here comes the wind, with a noise and a whirr,
Out on the streets he is making a stir.
Now he sends flying a fine, stiff hat,
Tosses and leaves it all muddy and flat.
Turns an umbrella quite inside out,
Tears up stray papers and scatters about,
Makes big balloons out of ladies' long capes,
Skirts into sails, then the queerest of shapes.
The wind is an enemy, often we say:
"We never quite like it—a windy day!"

The wind blows the seeds from their close little pods
And scatters them far away—rods upon rods;
He plants them where never an eye could see
Place for their growing and blooming to be.
He blows away rain, and scatters the dew,
He sweeps the earth clean and makes it all new.
He blows away sickness and brings good health
He comes over laden with beauty and wealth.
Oh, the wind is a friend! Let us always say:
"We love it! We love it!—a windy day!"

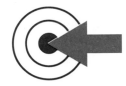

Personification

Personification is a figure of speech in which an animal, object, or idea is given human qualities. In "Wind Song," the wind is given human qualities: He "plants," "sweeps," and "tears up stray papers."

Personification is one tool authors use to make their writing more lively and interesting. Think of ways you can use personification to improve your own writing.

MULTIPLE-CHOICE GUIDED PRACTICE

Directions: Choose the best answer for each question. Then check yourself with the answers provided below each question.

1. What information does the author use to support the opinion that the wind is an enemy?

    A the wind blows seeds around

    B the wind blows the rain away

    C the wind blows sickness away

    D the wind turns umbrellas inside out

This question asks you to recall details from the poem. Skim (look quickly through) the poem to find the section containing the details needed to answer the question. Then, reread that section carefully. Choices **A, B,** and **C** are all ways that the wind is a friend. Choice **D** is the only possible answer because a friend would not turn umbrellas inside out.

2. This poem is probably trying to

   F share the good and bad things about the wind

   G teach the reader about our enemy, the wind

   H entertain the reader with stories about the wind

   J remind people to be careful with their umbrellas

In the poem, the wind is described as *both* a friend and an enemy. The only answer that reflects both is **F**.

3. The author uses the pronoun "he" in the poem to refer to

   A the man who lost his hat

   B the wind

   C the gardener who plants seeds

   D the friend

The poem begins with a description of the wind: "Here comes the wind, with a noise and a whirr, / Out on the streets he is making a stir. / Now he sends flying a fine, stiff hat" (lines 1–3). Wind can be noisy and it can blow things such as hats around. The correct answer is the wind, choice **B**.

4. According to the poem, what does the wind leave all muddy and flat?

   F hat

   G balloons

   H umbrella

   J papers

Skim the poem to "find and recall the details" to answer this question. The correct answer, which is choice **F**, is found in lines 3 and 4 of the poem.

5. How does the wind bring good health?

   A it blows away the rain

   B sweeps the earth clean

   C blows away sickness

   D blows seeds around

Skim the poem. Then find and reread the section of the poem containing the answer: "He blows away sickness and brings good health" (line 17). The correct answer is **C**.

6. When the author states that "the wind is a friend," he probably means

   F the wind blew the hat back

   G the wind can be helpful

   H the wind is usually noisy

   J the wind blows papers around

In the second stanza, the author describes some of the good, helpful things that the wind may do. Choices **F**, **H**, and **J** describe the wind as more of an enemy. The correct answer is **G**.

Directions: Read the American tale about two old friends. Then answer questions 7 through 12.

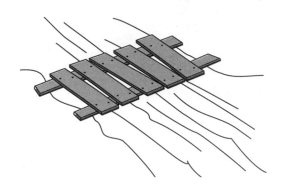

Old Joe and the Carpenter

An American Tale

Old Joe lived in the country. His lifelong neighbor was his best friend. Their children were grown and their wives were gone; they had only each other and their farms.

One day, they had a serious disagreement over a stray calf. It was found on a neighbor's land and both of them claimed it. The two men were stubborn and would not give in. They went back to their farms and stayed there. Weeks went by without a word between them.

Old Joe was feeling poorly when he heard a knock at his front door. At first, he thought it was his neighbor. When he opened the door, he was surprised to see a stranger. The man introduced himself as a "carpenter." He carried a toolbox and had kind eyes.

He explained that he was looking for work. Old Joe said he had a job or two for the carpenter. He showed the man his neighbor's house. There was a new creek running between the two pieces of property, freshly dug by Old Joe's neighbor, to separate their property.

Old Joe asked the carpenter to build a fence on his property so that he would not have to look at the creek. He helped the carpenter get started and then went to get more supplies for the fence. The carpenter worked without rest and finished the job all by himself.

When Old Joe returned and saw what the carpenter had built, he was speechless. The carpenter hadn't built a fence; he had built a bridge. The bridge reached from one side of the creek to the other.

Old Joe's neighbor crossed the bridge; he was quick to apologize for their misunderstanding. He told Old Joe that he could have the calf. They shook hands and thanked the carpenter for his work. Both of them suggested he stay and complete other jobs they had for him.

The carpenter declined the work and said he had to leave; he had more bridges to build.

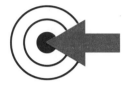

Symbolism

A **symbol** is a word or object that stands for something else. Writers sometimes use a symbol when they want to suggest a deeper meaning, a meaning beyond what the words themselves seem to say. Think of symbols we see every day, such as a flag, rose, and heart. The American flag itself is just a piece of cloth, but it makes us think of our country, America. A rose is a type of flower, and a heart is an organ, but they frequently stand for love. The tale "Old Joe and the Carpenter" uses the symbols of the fence and the bridge.

MULTIPLE-CHOICE GUIDED PRACTICE

7. Whom did Old Joe expect to see or think he would see when he heard a knock at the door?

  A his neighbor

  B his children

  C a carpenter

  D his wife

Skim the tale until you find the answer. Reread the section containing the answer (paragraph 3). This question is tricky. Old Joe thought that he would see his neighbor, but he saw a carpenter instead. The correct answer is choice **A.**

8. The last sentence of the tale begins as follows: "The carpenter declined the work..." What does the word "declined" mean in that sentence?

F showed

G expected

H refused

J was grateful for

A clue to the word's meaning is found in the rest of the sentence. Reread the last sentence of the tale. After declining more work, the carpenter told Old Joe and his friend that he had to leave. The answer is **H**. The word "decline" means to refuse or turn down.

9. What happens "right after" both Old Joe and his neighbor claimed the stray calf?

A the neighbor dug a creek

B both men stopped speaking to one another

C they met a carpenter

D Old Joe decided he needed a fence

This question asks you to recall the sequence of events in the tale. The "sequence of events" refers to the order in which things happen in a selection. All of the events happened after Old Joe and his neighbor claimed the calf. Reread the tale to find the event that happened "right after." The correct answer is **B**.

10. Why was the disagreement over the calf so serious for the two men?

F their wives were gone

G they both needed the calf

H they wanted to be right

J they had only each other

All of the choices listed are possible reasons for a disagreement, but you need to choose the best answer based on information and details provided in the tale. The best answer for this question is **J**.

11. When the carpenter built a bridge rather than the fence that Old Joe had requested, why wasn't Old Joe upset?

   A he changed his mind

   B he got his friend back

   C he didn't have enough materials for a fence

   D he liked the better view of the creek

Old Joe was pleased because he did get his friend back, so the answer is **B**. There is no information in the tale to support the other letter choices.

12. What do you think the carpenter meant when he said that he had more bridges to build?

   F he has more friendships to build

   G he doesn't like to do other jobs

   H he doesn't like to build fences

   J he has more creeks to cross

You need to think about the fence and the bridge as symbols. Fences separate people and things, but bridges connect. The correct answer is **F**. This carpenter is building or repairing (fixing) a relationship.

Directions: Read the poem about Mr. Nobody. Then answer questions 13 through 17.

Mr. Nobody

Anonymous

I know a funny little man,
As quiet as a mouse,
Who does the mischief that is done
In everybody's house!
There's no one ever sees his face,
And yet we all agree
That every plate we break was cracked
By Mr. Nobody.

'Tis he who always tears our books,
Who leaves the door ajar,
He pulls the buttons from our shirts,
And scatters pins afar;
That squeaking door will always squeak,
For, prithee, don't you see,
We leave the oiling to be done
By Mr. Nobody.

The finger marks upon the door
By none of us are made;
We never leave the blinds unclosed,
To let the curtains fade.
The ink we never spill; the boots
That lying round you see
Are not our boots—they all belong
To Mr. Nobody.

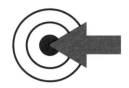

Imagery

Writers sometimes use "images" (mental pictures) to help the reader see pictures or feel sensations without actually experiencing them. In "Mr. Nobody," the poet creates a picture of a house where many things happen and no one takes responsibility.

Similes

Authors use similes to make their writing more descriptive and entertaining. A simile is a figure of speech that compares two different things using the words "like" or "as." In "Mr. Nobody" (lines 1 and 2), the poet compares the funny, little man to a quiet mouse. Try to use similes in your own writing so that it will be "as amusing as a carnival ride" (another simile).

MULTIPLE-CHOICE GUIDED PRACTICE

13. What is the main idea of the poem?

   A a stranger keeps sneaking into everyone's house

   B Mr. Nobody is a strange neighbor

   C a funny little man gets into mischief

   D everyone blames Mr. Nobody instead of taking the blame themselves

The main idea is the big idea: It's what a selection (a poem in this case) is mostly about. Read the poem carefully. Choices **A, B,** and **C** do not indicate the main (most important) idea of the poem. The correct answer is **D.**

14. According to the poem, what does Mr. Nobody do?

F   oils a squeaky door

G   leaves finger marks

H   repairs torn books

J   sews buttons on shirts

Read the question, answer choices, and poem carefully. Mr. Nobody does not oil the door; it will always squeak so choice **F** is incorrect. He tears books and pulls buttons off shirts so choices **H** and **J** are also incorrect. The correct answer is **G**: Mr. Nobody is blamed for leaving finger marks.

15. The next time something is broken or misplaced, everyone will probably blame

A   the littlest member of the family

B   Mr. Nobody

C   everybody else

D   a mouse

This question asks you to predict what will happen next in the poem. The details given in the poem, including the poem's title, provide clues that will help you make a good guess. According to the poem, no one takes responsibility for the things that happen in the house. Mr. Nobody must be responsible. The best answer is **B**.

16. According to the poem, Mr. Nobody does all of the mischief that is done. What does mischief mean?

   F kindness

   G goodness

   H trouble

   J niceness

Mr. Nobody is responsible for all of the "trouble" that happens around the house, so letter choices **F**, **G**, and **J** are incorrect. A synonym (a word that means the same as or nearly the same as) for *mischief* would be the word trouble, choice **H**.

17. The author of the poem tells us that Mr. Nobody is unknown to everyone because

   A he is as quiet as a mouse

   B he is a funny little man

   C no one ever sees his face

   D he always tears our books

All of the letter choices are details given in the poem. The only one that shows he is unknown would be that "no one ever sees his face," choice **C**.

Directions: Read the story about teddy bears, and then answer questions 18 through 22.

Who Put the "Teddy" in Teddy Bear?

Source: *The Washington Post,* Clifford K. Berryman, 1902.

In 1902 America's then-president, Theodore "Teddy" Roosevelt, visited Mississippi to settle a disagreement between Mississippi and its neighboring state, Louisiana. While in the south, he went bear hunting with some of his friends and aides. His hunting party was joined by a group of newspaper reporters.

Members hunted for a few days, but they didn't capture any bears. Finally, on the last day of the hunt, Roosevelt's friends cornered a bear cub and presented it to the president as a sitting target. Teddy Roosevelt chose not to shoot the helpless animal: "Spare the bear. I will not shoot a tethered animal!" he exclaimed. A cartoonist, Clifford Berryman, either heard about or witnessed the president's act; he drew a black and white cartoon showing how the president refused to shoot the bear. This cartoon appeared in newspapers all over the country.

One married couple, the Michtoms, from Brooklyn, New York, saw the cartoon and was inspired by the president's action, or lack of action. Morris Michtom's wife created a stuffed bear with movable arms and legs. She and her husband placed the bears in the window of their candy store with a copy of the cartoon. The "Teddy" bears were a hit. The Michtoms wrote the president and received permission to use his name. The popularity of the teddy bears spread and soon they were being created in Germany as well.

Teddy bears are over 100 years old and are still popular with many children and adults. They are collected by many people; stamps and coins are the only items collected more.

MULTIPLE-CHOICE GUIDED PRACTICE

18. According to the article, Teddy Roosevelt became famous for something he did not do. What was it?

F go bear hunting

G like cartoons

H become president

J shoot a small bear

Read the question carefully. Teddy Roosevelt was famous for NOT shooting the little bear. The correct answer is **J**.

19. After seeing the cartoon, people thought that President Roosevelt was

A lucky

B kind

C frightened

D mean

The President chose not to shoot the bear. Most people would think he was kind for making that choice. The correct answer is **B**.

20. Which detail from the story is proof of the teddy bear's popularity?

    F there was a cartoon drawn

    G the president went hunting for bears

    H teddy bears were stuffed, with moveable arms

    J teddy bears were copied by other toy makers

When something is "liked" by most people, then that something is considered to be popular. Answers **F** and **G** are about real bears. Answer **H** refers to construction of the bears. The only answer that is proof of popularity is **J**.

21. When did the events described in this story take place?

    A more than 200 years ago

    B about 60 years ago

    C about 30 years ago

    D about a century ago

President Roosevelt went on his now-famous bear hunt in Mississippi in 1902, which is about 100 years ago. Therefore, choices **A**, **B**, and **C** are not correct. A century equals a period of 100 years, so the correct answer is choice **D**. If you did not know the meaning of the word "century," you could have still figured out this answer by eliminating the other choices, which you knew were obviously incorrect. That's what "making a good guess" is about.

22. The story states that the Michtoms were *inspired* by the cartoon.
What does the word *inspired* mean?

F influenced

G taught

H able

J chosen

Read the sentence in the third paragraph containing the vocabulary word "inspired." Also, read the sentence "before" and the sentence "after" the word to decide which of the letter choices makes sense. After seeing the cartoon, Mrs. Michtom created a stuffed bear. The word "inspired" means to influence someone to do something (make teddy bears in this case). The correct answer is **F**.

Directions: Read the Chinese tale below. Then answer questions 23 through 28.

The Nightingale

A Chinese Tale

Long ago, in the far-off land of China, deep in the forest, there lived a nightingale. The nightingale sang a song so beautiful that the other animals of the forest would stop to listen to her sing.

Nightingale: Tra-la-lee! Tra-la-lee! La-la-tra-la-lee!

Emperor: Who is that singing? That is the most beautiful singing I have ever heard! Servants come here at once!

Servant 1: Yes, mighty emperor?

Servant 2: What can we do for you?

Emperor: Do you hear that singing?

Nightingale: Tra-la-lee! Tra-la-lee!

Servant 1: Yes, it is lovely.

Emperor: Well, I must have it! Please find whoever is singing and bring him or her to me. We will dine together.

So the servants went off to find the singer. They listened to every animal they met. They listened to the cow, "Moo." They listened to the frogs, "Rib-bit." They walked deeper and deeper into the forest until at last they heard," Tra-la-lee! Tra-la-lee!"

Servant 1: There she is, a small gray bird.

Servant 2: I don't believe it. Such beautiful music from such a plain-looking bird.

Servant 1: Miss Nightingale, our emperor loves your singing. He has sent us to invite you for dinner.

Nightingale: It would be a pleasure. Tra-la-lee. Let's go to the palace.

They arrived at the palace. The emperor had a special feast prepared and many people came to hear the nightingale's song.

Emperor: My dear nightingale, please sing for us.

Nightingale: Tra-la-lee! Tra-la-lee!

The emperor did enjoy the song. He loved it so much that he decided to keep the nightingale guarded in a beautiful cage. Soon, the nightingale grew homesick. One day, the emperor received a golden toy bird as a present. It was encrusted in diamonds and was the most beautiful thing he had ever seen. It would sing a beautiful song when it was wound up. Everyone was so interested in the toy bird that the nightingale was able to open her cage and fly away.

Emperor: Don't worry; we have a new bird to sing songs.

Servant 1: But the toy bird sings the same song.

After a year, the toy bird broke. The emperor became very sick in his quiet palace.

Emperor: I need music to help me feel better. I think I hear music coming from outside.

Nightingale: Tra-la-lee! Tra-la-lee!

Emperor: You have returned to sing to me! Nightingale, I have missed you! How can I ever repay you?

Nightingale: Your smile and good health are payment enough. You can do one more thing for me.

Emperor: Anything!

Nightingale: I cannot live in the palace. I need to live in the forest, my home. I will visit you often.

The emperor promised, so the nightingale returned nightly to sing to the emperor.

No one ever knew the nightingale was the best medicine.

> encrusted:
> covered or
> coated in

MULTIPLE-CHOICE GUIDED PRACTICE

23. Why did the emperor need to find the bird?

  A he wanted to fill the cage

  B he wanted to stop the singing

  C he wanted to keep healthy

  D he liked the songs of the nightingale

Skim the poem to find and recall the details to answer this question. Reread those details carefully. As Servant 1 says in the poem, "Miss Nightingale, our emperor loves your singing." The correct answer is **D**.

24. What surprised the servants when they located the nightingale?

  F it sang a beautiful song

  G it lived deep in the forest

  H it was a plain bird

  J it was the most beautiful bird they had ever seen

As Servant 2 stated, "I don't believe it. Such beautiful music from such a plain-looking bird." The correct answer is **H**.

25. How did the nightingale feel about singing for the Emperor "at first?"

  A the nightingale liked to make the emperor smile

  B the nightingale liked living in the beautiful palace

  C the nightingale liked the beautiful cage

  D the nightingale didn't like being in the palace

This is a question about the sequencing of events in the tale. Read the question carefully. Pay attention to the words "at first." The nightingale's feelings changed. In the beginning, she enjoyed making the emperor smile with her songs. The correct answer is **A**.

26. What was the most likely reason that the emperor had the nightingale guarded?

   F he needed to hear the songs of the nightingale

   G he cared for the nightingale

   H he wanted to be sure the nightingale stayed in the cage

   J he wanted to keep the nightingale happy

The best answer to explain why the nightingale was "guarded" is choice **H**. The other choices do make some sense, but they do not explain the most likely reason for having the nightingale guarded.

27. What lesson do you think the emperor learned from his experience with the nightingale?

   A never try to keep a bird in a cage

   B songs will keep you healthy

   C you need to treat someone well if you care for him or her

   D it is better to have a toy bird than a live bird

Lessons taught by tales are usually life lessons or important lessons to live by. All of the above choices are lessons that may have been learned. The most important "life lesson" learned is letter choice **C**.

28. Why did the nightingale fly away from the palace?

    F she was jealous of the toy bird

    G the door of the cage was open

    H she didn't like the song of the toy bird

    J she wanted to return to the forest

According to the tale, the nightingale was homesick and wished to return home to the forest. The best answer is **J**.

Chapter 2

LISTENING

OVERVIEW: SESSION 2

The shaded box in the chart below shows what you will be asked to do in Session 2 on Day 2 of the test.

New York State English Language Arts Test		
Day 1	Day 2	Day 3
Session 1 45 minutes Multiple-Choice Section ■ Read 4–5 selections. ■ Answer 28 questions.	Session 2 45 minutes Listening Section ■ 2 short answers ■ 1 long response	Session 3 60 minutes Reading and Writing ■ Read 2 selections. ■ Write 3 short answers, 1–2 on each of the selections read. ■ Write 1 long response based on both reading selections.

The practice listening exercises in this book are designed to help you become a better listener, note taker, and writer. Listening is a skill you will use throughout your life. In the world around you, people perform tasks that require good listening skills. Doctors listen to their patients to heal them. Mechanics listen to customers to fix their cars. A waitress listens to customers' orders to serve the correct food.

You listen every day to directions and information presented in your classroom. You also listen to carry on conversations with your friends. Sometimes, a conflict arises between people simply because someone was not listening properly.

Being a better listener requires more than good hearing. You must remember information and be able to think about what you have heard.

LISTENING TIPS

- You will have 45 minutes to complete this part of the exam.
- Take no more than 1–2 minutes after the selection is read to complete your notes.
- Take 10–15 minutes to write the two short answers.
- Use the last 20–30 minutes to write the long response.
- Write about what you have listened to and read.

Your writing on the ELA will be scored on:

- how well you organize and communicate your thoughts
- how completely and correctly you answer all parts of the question
- how clearly you use details and examples to fully support your ideas
- how pleasurable and interesting your writing is
- how accurately you use spelling, grammar, punctuation, and paragraphing

Use one or both of the following to check your writing:

■ the Student Checklist on page 54 (last page of this chapter).
■ the more detailed Listening/Writing Rubric, which can be found in Chapter 4 on pages 96–99.

LISTENING TIPS TO KEEP YOU ON TARGET

■ Prepare for listening by removing distractions (such as scraps of paper).
■ Stop moving, touching, and talking.
■ Tune out distracting sounds.
■ Focus on the speaker (eye contact).
■ Think about what is being said.
■ Try to form a picture in your head of what the speaker is saying.
■ Pay very close attention to both readings.
■ During the second reading, take notes on the most important details.

If the selection read aloud is a story, listen for and try to write down the following story elements in your notes:

1. title/author

2. setting

3. important characters

   —what do they look like?

   —how do they act?

   —why do they act a certain way?

4. conflict (problem in the story)

5. sequence of main events (beginning, middle, and end)

6. resolution or lesson learned

If the passage read aloud is not a story, listen for and try to write down the following:

1. title/author

2. important ideas and details

3. why the author is writing the selection (example: to describe or explain something, to convince)

4. people, animals, and places

   ■ Use single word notes and phrases, abbreviations, and/or pictures/symbols to save time.
   ■ You may want to organize details in a graphic organizer such as a chart, diagram, story map, or list.

LISTENING

Directions: In this section of the test, a selection will be read aloud to you twice. Please listen carefully each time you hear the selection because you will then be asked to answer specific questions about the selection.

You will listen to the story twice. **Do not take notes during the first reading.**

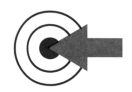

During the first reading, listen carefully for main ideas and details. Think about the story elements: title, setting, characters, conflict (problem), sequence of events to solution, and resolution (solution).

You may take notes during the second reading using the space provided.

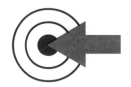

Between the first and second reading, you may want to create some type of graphic organizer to help you organize your notes.

During the second reading, begin to take notes about the most important details in the selection. Write only key words or phrases to remember the details. When taking notes, do **not** write in complete sentences. Your notes should answer questions about the story elements.

You may refer back to your notes to answer the questions that follow. **Your notes will not count toward your end score.**

When the second reading is finished, fill in the necessary details. Don't spend too much time on your notes page. Refer back to your notes during writing. You will need to use details from the selection in your writing.

GUIDED PRACTICE

LISTENING PRACTICE 1

Directions: In this section of the test, a story called "A Village of Listeners" will be read aloud to you twice. Please listen carefully each time the story is read because you will then be asked to answer specific questions about the story.

During the first reading, listen closely but do not take notes. You may take notes during the second reading. Please use the space provided below for your notes. You may refer back to your notes to answer the questions that follow. Your notes will *not* count toward your score.

Notes

A Village of Listeners

There once was a village where no one listened. Everyone talked and everyone could hear, but no one listened. When villagers ordered pancakes at the local restaurant, the waitress brought them chocolate cake instead. Often, firemen and policemen went to the wrong address because they didn't listen carefully to the address of the emergency. Things were usually in a state of confusion in this rural community.

At village meetings people talked, but sadly no one listened. Everyone wanted to share personal ideas and opinions, but didn't want to listen to anyone else's. There was always more fighting than cooperation. Nothing ever seemed to get accomplished in this village.

One day, a wise man visited and spoke to the hearts of the villagers. He advised them to clear their minds, focus on the other people around them, and value what others had to say. The wise man asked people to work together and have real conversations that required more listening than talking.

Soon, the village buzzed with cooperation. People were happier and safer; problems were solved. The villagers taught their children to be better listeners so that the village would continue to be wiser for generations to come.

NOTE TAKING

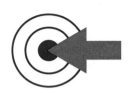

Write down key words or phrases, which summarize the order of events in a selection. Do **not** try to write down every word you hear. Take notes on only the most important details.

You can save time and write down more information if you use abbreviations and symbols during note taking. Think about and practice using abbreviations and symbols that will work for you, such as "bec." to stand for *because,* or a * to show that the information is super important.

Like the athlete who needs to practice for an upcoming sports events, you can improve your skill in note taking by practicing. A good time to practice taking notes is when your teacher is giving a lesson.

The sample response below uses the following abbreviations and symbols: choc. for *chocolate* and & for *and.* It is written using words and phrases, rather than complete sentences.

SEQUENCE OF EVENTS

How many of these details did you record during listening?

village
no one listened
pancakes—choc. cake
firemen & policemen—wrong address
confusion
meetings—no one listening
fighting
nothing gets done
wise man—spoke to hearts
focus on others
listen
cooperating
happier, safer, problems solved
teach children to listen
brighter future

GRAPHIC ORGANIZER FOR UNDERSTANDING STORY ELEMENTS

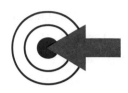

Simple notes can be arranged in a story web using details from the story.

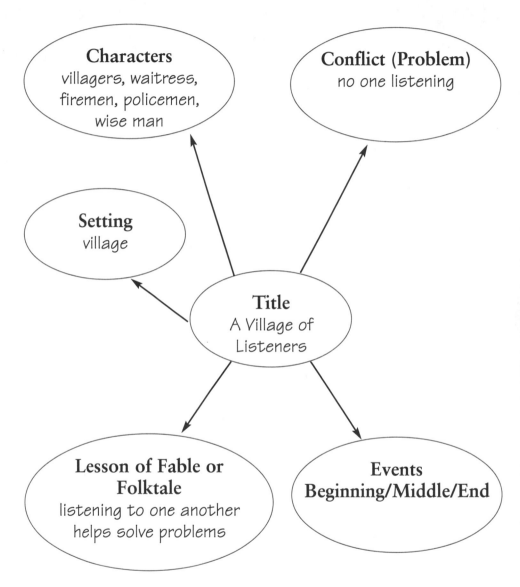

Characters
villagers, waitress, firemen, policemen, wise man

Conflict (Problem)
no one listening

Setting
village

Title
A Village of Listeners

Lesson of Fable or Folktale
listening to one another helps solve problems

Events
Beginning/Middle/End

Use at least 2 to 3 details from the story in your answer. You need to show that you are a good listener and that you understood the story.

BEGINNING, MIDDLE, AND END ORGANIZER

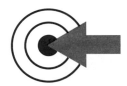

Directions: Use your notes to help you complete the chart below.

SETTING Where and when the story takes place	
BEGINNING What happens at the beginning of the story? Readers meet the characters. The conflict begins.	
MIDDLE What happens in the middle of the story? The characters and the conflict are described in more detail.	
END What happens at the end of the story? The problem is somehow solved.	

Remember that the beginning of the story introduces the problem. The end of the story should tell the resolution of the problem.

Sample Completed Chart

SETTING Where and when the story takes place	in a village, a long time ago
BEGINNING What happens at the beginning of the story? Readers meet the characters. The conflict begins.	Villagers do not listen to one another.
MIDDLE What happens in the middle of the story? The characters and the conflict are described in more detail.	Waitress served the wrong food. Firemen and policemen go to wrong address. Wise man visits village. He tells people to start listening to one another.
END What happens at the end of the story? The problem is somehow solved.	Villagers start to listen to one another. They begin to solve problems and are happier. They teach their children to be good listeners so they can solve future problems.

The village in the story has many problems. What causes most of the problems? Use examples from the story.

Planning Space

Answer

_____

_____

_____

_____

_____

_____

_____

_____

CAUSE AND EFFECT

When one event makes another event happen, the first is the cause and the second is the event.

The cause-effect chart below shows what happens in the village as a result of people not listening to each other.

Cause (event that happened first)	Effects (event that happened second)
People in the village do not listen to one another.	The entire village was in a state of confusion. Many problems could not get solved. A waitress served the wrong food. Firemen and policemen go to wrong address.

Sample Response

The response below includes a **topic sentence** that reflects or restates the question. A topic sentence states the main (big) idea of a paragraph. The response also includes 3 examples from the selection that support the answer given.

Most of the problems in the village were caused by people not listening to one another. The waitress in the restaurant served the wrong food to customers because she did not listen carefully. She served chocolate cake, but the customer had ordered pancakes. Firemen and policemen went to the wrong addresses for emergencies because they didn't listen carefully. The problems were caused and could not be solved because no one listened to anyone else.

WRITING ABOUT CHANGE

Describe how the village changed from the beginning to the end of the story. Write your answer using details from the story.

In your answer, be sure to:
- describe the village at the beginning of the story.
- tell what caused the village to change.
- explain how the village is different at the end of the story.
- use specific details from the story.
- check your writing for correct spelling, grammar, capitalization, and punctuation.

Planning Space

_____

_____

_____

_____

_____

_____

_____

_____

_____

_____

_____

_____

Did you use a graphic organizer to help you plan your answer?

T-CHART

Below is a two-column list known as a T-chart. The list helps organize details to show how the village changed. It shows you the differences between the village at the beginning of the story and the village at the end of the story.

Sample T-Chart

Village at beginning of story (before the wise man)	Village at end of story (after the wise man)
People talk; no one listens	People have conversations
Things confused—	More listening than talking
restaurant orders,	People happier
emergency addresses	Taught children to listen
More fighting than teamwork	Problems solved
Could not solve problems	

Sample Response

The village changed greatly from the beginning to the end of the story. It changed for the better, thanks to the visit from a wise man.

At the beginning of "A Village of Listeners," the villagers did not listen to each other. The whole community was in a state of confusion. Restaurant orders were not made correctly, and the firemen and policemen sometimes went to the wrong address because they did not listen carefully. This village had more problems than a math book. Problems could not get solved because everyone was talking a mile a minute all at the same time.

One day, a wise man visited the village. Surprisingly, the villagers stopped talking long enough to listen to the wise man. He told the villagers to listen to others. They followed his advice, and began to talk less and listen to each other more. Problems could now get solved, and children would be taught the importance of listening. The community was now a more cheerful place.

LISTENING PRACTICE II

Directions: In this section of the test, a story called "A Little, Big Man" will be read aloud to you twice. Please listen carefully each time the story is read because you will then be asked to answer specific questions about the story.

During the first reading, listen closely but do not take notes. You may take notes during the second reading. Please use the space provided below for your notes. You may refer back to your notes to answer the questions that follow. Your notes will not count toward your score.

Notes

A Little, Big Man

Once there lived a little man. He wished he would grow to be taller, but he did not grow at all. As the years passed, the only thing that grew was his disappointment. He decided to ask others for advice.

One day the little man approached a bull. He asked the bull how to become bigger. The bull tossed his head and said, "Eat lots of grass and hay and spend all day lying down. That is how I became as big as I am."

The little man went home and ate lots of grass and hay and spent the day lying around. He did not grow. He got a stomachache from the hay and grass, and a backache from lying down all day.

The little man decided to ask the horse for advice. The horse suggested he eat oats and straw, and get plenty of exercise running around.

The man went home and followed the horse's directions. He didn't grow an inch. He got sick from the oats and straw and his legs were sore from all the running.

The little man was ready to give up when he decided to consult the wisest creature in the forest. When he asked the owl for advice to grow taller, the owl wanted to know why he wanted to be taller.

The man explained that he wanted to see more. The owl suggested he climb a tree. The man was surprised by the idea and embarrassed that the solution could be so simple.

He thanked the owl and, as he was about to leave, the owl left him with this thought, "If a man has a brain and uses it, it doesn't matter what size he is; he is big enough for anything."

TIPS FOR UNDERSTANDING THE MEANING OF QUOTATIONS

- Review your notes for any information that may help explain the quotation.
- Name the character(s) involved.
- Restate the quotation using different words.

Complete the chart below using details from the story.

Quotation	Meaning
As the years passed, the only thing that grew was his disappointment.	
If a man has a brain and uses it, it doesn't matter what size he is; he is big enough for anything.	

Sample Completed Chart

Quotation	Meaning
As the years passed, the only thing that grew was his disappointment.	For a long time, the little man wished he would grow taller. He was very sad that he couldn't grow and he became sadder and sadder.
If a man has a brain and uses it, it doesn't matter what size he is; he is big enough for anything.	The owl's advice was that if people think with their brain, then they can solve any problem. They can overcome being small by using their brain power.

Why do you think the horse and the bull gave the little man the advice they did?

- Begin with a topic sentence. A topic sentence tells what the rest of the paragraph is about.
- Then give at least 3 details to answer the question and to show your understanding of what you heard.

_____

_____

_____

_____

_____

_____

_____

_____

_____

Sample Response

The horse and bull gave the little man advice about growing taller. The advice they gave was what had worked for them. The bull knew that he grew when he ate grass and hay, and spent the day lying down. The horse knew that he grew when he ate oats and straw, and ran around. Their advice didn't work for the little man.

ANSWERING ALL PARTS OF THE QUESTION

- Read the question carefully.
- Pay attention to each bullet.
- Put a check next to each bullet answered.
- Read your writing to be sure you have answered all parts of the question.

Tell how the little man changed from the beginning to the end of the story.

In your answer, be sure to:

- describe the little man at the beginning of the story.
- tell what caused him to change.
- explain how he is different at the end of the story.
- use specific details from the story.
- check your writing for correct spelling, grammar, capitalization, and punctuation.

Planning Space

LISTENING PRACTICE III

Directions: In this section of the test, a story called "Dr. Jane Goodall" will be read aloud to you twice. Please listen carefully each time the story is read because you will then be asked to answer specific questions about the story.

During the first reading, listen closely but do not take notes. You may take notes during the second reading. Please use the space provided below for your notes. You may refer back to your notes to answer the questions that follow. Your notes will not count toward your score.

Notes

Dr. Jane Goodall

Jane Goodall loved and cared for animals from the time she was a young girl. One of her favorite toys was a stuffed chimpanzee, which was given to her by her father. Her favorite childhood books were about animals. She was fond of Tarzan books and dreamed of adventures in Africa.

Her animal research can be traced back to her childhood. Jane was curious about how chickens are able to lay eggs. She waited quietly for hours in the hen house to witness a hen laying an egg. This curiosity and patience would later be helpful in her study of chimpanzees.

In her early twenties, Jane went to Africa to work, first as a secretary for a documentary film company. Next, she worked as an assistant for the famous Dr. Louis Leakey. He was impressed by her knowledge of Africa and its animals. Dr. Leaky gave her the opportunity to live her dream of

studying and working with animals. Jane lived with, played with, and studied the chimpanzees. She made many new discoveries about chimpanzees. She watched them make a tool from a branch to catch termites. Dr. Goodall wrote books and helped produce documentaries to share her discoveries with others.

Jane Goodall's childhood love has become a lifelong passion. Today, she speaks to children around the world about caring for the environment and the creatures living in it.

TIME ORDER WORDS

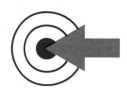

Look for clue words or phrases that will help you understand the events of a selection in the order in which they happened. Below are some time order words from "Dr. Jane Goodall":

- from the time she was a young girl
- this curiosity and patience would "later" be helpful
- in her early twenties
- today

TIMELINE CHART

Dr. Jane Goodall is a famous humanitarian and scientist. Create a timeline with information from the selection.

Time in the Life of Dr. Goodall	Event
Childhood	
When she was in her twenties...	
Today	

Time in the Life of Dr. Goodall	Event
Childhood	She watched a chicken lay an egg.
When she was in her twenties...	She went to Africa to study chimpanzees.
Today	She speaks to children around the world about caring for the environment and the creatures in it.

Time Order Words and Phrases

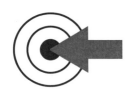

Time order words and phrases help you understand the events of a selection in the order in which they happened.

in the beginning (middle, end)	shortly	earlier
first	soon	when
second	as soon as	while
then	before	at the end
next	later	finally
after	during	at last
after a while	now	until
after that	by the time	in the meantime
afterward	at that time	meanwhile
	immediately	in the past

Exact time order words and phrases, such as:

days of the week—on Wednesday, after Monday, before Saturday

months—last February, next October

hours—at noon, by six o'clock

dates and years—July 4, 1776

In the article about Dr. Jane Goodall, the author wrote, "This curiosity and patience would later be helpful in her study of chimpanzees." What do you think this statement means?

Sometimes it helps to break a question into parts.

- This curiosity and patience—Dr. Goodall was always curious and patient.
- Would later be helpful—She was curious and patient as a child and would later use those skills in her work. She would question and search for answers in her research.

Sample Response

Ever since she was a little girl, Dr. Jane Goodall was always curious and patient. She would use both of these traits in her work, later in her life.

When she was young, Dr. Goodall was very interested in learning how chickens laid eggs. She spent hours waiting in the hen house to see the event take place.

In her adult life, Dr. Goodall was curious about chimpanzees. She spent years patiently observing their behavior in the wild. Her curiosity made her question the things around her and search for answers. Dr. Goodall's patience would help her spend much time trying to find the answers.

Your answer may be correct if you have at least 3 details from the story to support your answer.

1. She was curious about chickens laying eggs.

2. She waited patiently in the hen house to observe the hens laying eggs.

3. As an adult she was curious about chimpanzees.

4. She patiently observed chimpanzees' behavior and made discoveries.

5. She watched chimpanzees make tools to catch termites.

Dr. Goodall's lifelong love could be traced back to her childhood.

1. What was that love?

2. How did it change over time?

3. Be sure to include examples from the article.

_____

_____

_____

_____

_____

_____

_____

_____

_____

_____

_____

Sample Response

Dr. Goodall's lifelong love of animals can be traced back to her childhood. She loved and cared for animals even as a young girl. Her favorite books were about animals and African adventures. During her childhood, Dr. Goodall was interested in how chickens were able to lay eggs.

As an adult, she lived in Africa doing chimpanzee research. Today, she speaks to children around the world about caring for the environment and animals.

Details from the listening selection:

1. Her favorite toy as a child was a stuffed chimpanzee.
2. She liked Tarzan books.
3. She observed animals as a child.
4. She watched a hen lay eggs.
5. She was always curious about animal behavior.
6. As an adult, she studied animals in Africa.
7. She made new discoveries about chimpanzees.
8. She wrote books about animals.
9. She still shares her love of animals with children today.
10. She writes and speaks about caring for animals and their environment.

Your answer should have at least 3 details that show her lifelong love of animals and how it changed over time.

STUDENT CHECKLIST

Meaning

> Did you complete the task by answering all the bulleted items in the question?
>
> Did you make connections and show you thought about the text read aloud?

Development

> Did you use specific examples and important details from the selection to support your ideas?
>
> Did you explain your answer fully?

Organization

> Did you begin with a topic sentence, an introduction to your writing?
>
> Did you use signal words to help with the direction of your writing?

Ideas and Language Use

> Did you write with a purpose (to inform, entertain, persuade, describe) in mind?
>
> Did you use interesting language?

Conventions

> Did you check your spelling, punctuation, and grammar?
>
> Did you start every sentence with a capital and end every sentence with the correct punctuation?

CONNECTING READING AND WRITING

OVERVIEW: SESSION 3

The shaded column in the chart below shows what you will be asked to do in Session 3 on Day 3 of the test.

New York State English Language Arts Test		
Day 1	Day 2	Day 3
Session 1 45 minutes Multiple-Choice Section ■ Read 4–5 selections. ■ Answer 28 questions.	Session 2 45 minutes Listening Section ■ 2 short answers ■ 1 long response	Session 3 60 minutes Reading and Writing ■ Read 2 selections. ■ Write 3 short answers, 1–2 on each of the selections read. ■ Write 1 long response based on both reading selections.

You will have 60 minutes to finish this part of the exam.

- Reading the two selections should take about 15–20 minutes.
- Writing answers for each of the short responses should take about 5–10 minutes each.
- Organizing and writing the long response should take about 20 minutes.

TIPS FOR SUCCESS

The poem below will help you remember the steps needed for success on the ELA test.

RUBRIC

R is for **reading carefully twice,**

　　That is certainly the best advice.

U is for **understanding the question asked.**

　　Once you do, you are ready to start the task.

B is for **beginning with a topic sentence,** number one.

　　Be sure it answers the question when done.

R is for **real examples** you choose.

　　They're from the story and support ideas you use.

I is for **interesting, insightful connections.**

　　Think about important facts during reflections.

reflections: thoughts

C is for **concluding sentence** and organization that's clear.

　　Correct spelling, grammar, and punctuation; you have nothing to fear.

The chart below further explains the poem "RUBRIC." In some of the pages that follow, you will be asked to place a check next to each lettered section of the word rubric to show that you have completed the task required for that section.

R	Reading carefully	Read all information on the page: directions, captions, as well as the selection. READ AT LEAST TWICE.
U	Understanding the question	Read the question carefully. Be sure you understand it.
B	Beginning with a topic sentence	A topic sentence will get your answer started and focus the supporting details.
R	Real examples from the selection	Search the selection you have just read for examples that will support your answer.
I	Interesting, insightful connections	Think about what you have read. Make connections and build on the examples you use from the selection.
C	Conclusion and corrections	End with a concluding sentence. Then, go back and check your work for spelling, grammar, and punctuation. See the Appendix for more information.

GUIDED PRACTICE

R IS FOR READING CAREFULLY

Read all information carefully: introduction, headings, title, captions, and directions.

Directions: Below you will find the beginning part of a magazine article titled "Friendship." Read the article and then complete the Venn diagram.

Friendship

One day after swimming, nine-year-old Sammy Long found a bottle washed up on the beach near his home. When he discovered this note inside, he had no idea it would lead to a 10-year friendship.

Hello, Finder of This Bottle,

   Thank you for discovering this bottle and reading my note. I am an eleven-year-old girl, who lives on the island of Grand Turk in the Atlantic Ocean. Grand Turk is southeast of Florida and northeast of Cuba. It is a beautiful, warm, and sunny island. My home is very close to the beach, where I go often to walk and swim in the sparkling, blue ocean.
   I would like to have a pen pal as much as a coach would like to win a championship game. Please write back soon. Kindly send the letter to me at the following address: PO Box 22, Grand Turk, IH2237.

         Cheerfully,
         Helena Canti

Use the Venn diagram below to compare (tell how they are alike and how they are different) Helena and Sammy.

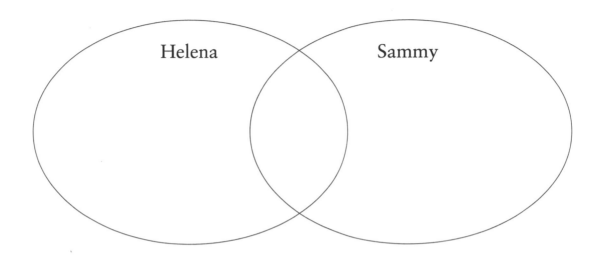

Helena   Sammy

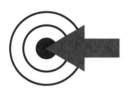

All the information about Sammy came from the introduction. To complete the Venn diagram, you had to read all information carefully.

U IS FOR UNDERSTANDING THE QUESTION ASKED

Look for key words in the question to help you understand the task.

Directions: Pretend you are Sammy. You have just found Helena's note and you are now going to write a letter to her. Use details from the article "Friendship" in your letter
  In your letter, be sure to:

- describe your discovery of the note.
- tell about yourself as Sammy.
- use at least 3 specific details from the article.

_____
Date

Dear Helena,

_____

_____

_____

_____

_____

_____

_____

_____

_____

Your new pen pal,
Sammy

Check your writing.

R	
U	
B	
R	
I	
C	

Did you READ CAREFULLY?

Did you UNDERSTAND THE QUESTION?

Did you BEGIN WITH A TOPIC SENTENCE?

Did you use REAL EXAMPLES FROM THE SELECTION?

Did you make INTERESTING, INSIGHTFUL CONNECTIONS?

Did you end with a CONCLUDING SENTENCE and make CORRECTIONS?

Did you do the following?

- Pretend you are Sammy and just found Helena's note.
- Write her a letter.
- Include details from the article "Friendship."
- Describe your discovery of the note.
- Tell about yourself as Sammy.
- Include at least 3 specific details from the article.

MORE ABOUT UNDERSTANDING THE QUESTION ASKED

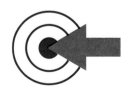

Underline important information in the task as a reminder of the details that must be included in your answer.

Underline key words in the task below. Be sure to use those details in your answer.

Pretend you are Sammy. You are going to write a letter to Helena. Use details from the article "Friendship" to recall how your friendship started more than 10 years ago.

Date

Dear Helena,

_____

_____

_____

_____

_____

_____

_____

_____

Your longtime buddy,
Sammy

Did you **read carefully?**

Did you **understand the question?**

R	
U	
B	
R	
I	
C	

B IS FOR BEGINNING WITH A TOPIC SENTENCE

A **topic sentence** is an opening sentence that tells the main idea of a paragraph.

Use clues in the question or task to help you write the topic sentence.

You have just read the magazine article "Friendship" (page 58) about people sending notes in bottles. You are concerned that bottles washing up on beaches around the world may be adding to our pollution problem. You decide to write a letter to the editor of the magazine expressing your concern.

Write only your topic sentence for the letter to the editor you will write.

_____

_____

_____

_____

After reading the magazine article "Friendship," you have decided to write a report about the island of Grand Turk. Use information from the article to start your report.

Write only your topic sentence for your report about Grand Turk.

_____

_____

_____

_____

R IS FOR REAL EXAMPLES TO SUPPORT YOUR ANSWER

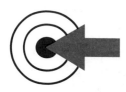

Be sure your examples support your answer and are from the reading.

The article "Friendship" describes two children who become friends.

Compare Helena and Sammy: Write a paragraph telling how they are alike and how they are different. Use details from the article. You may refer back to the Venn diagram activity on page 59.

_____

_____

_____

_____

_____

Use details from the article "Friendship" to write a paragraph describing the island of Grand Turk.

_____

_____

_____

_____

I IS FOR INTERESTING, INSIGHTFUL CONNECTIONS

Write about specific details from the story in your own words.

Showing insight means you use your own words and build on the details from the story. It is your own personal stamp on your answer.

The task below has 2 answers attached. Both answers are acceptable. One answer shows more insight. Which answer shows the most interesting, insightful details?

Question: Pretend you are Sammy. You have just found Helena's note and you are now going to write her a letter. Use details from "Friendship" in your letter.

Answer **A:**	The answer is acceptable. There are at least 3 details from the selection included.
Dear Helena,	
I am a nine-year-old boy who found your note in a bottle. You are only two years older than me so we should have things in common. Like you, I live near the beach.	
I would like to be your pen pal. Please write back soon.	
Sincerely, Sammy	

Question: Pretend you are Sammy. You have just found Helena's note and you are now going to write her a letter. Use details from "Friendship" in your letter.

Answer **B**:	
Dear Helena,	
I am a nine-year-old boy, who was pleasantly surprised when your floating note washed up on the beach near my house. Opening the bottle and reading the message inside was as thrilling as opening presents on my birthday. I have always wanted a pen pal and am very excited about writing to you.	The answer is acceptable. There are at least 3 details from the selection included.
The island of Grand Turk sounds delightful. Enjoy your walks on the beach and have fun swimming, but please don't forget to write me back.	
Hope to hear from you soon.	
Your pen pal, Sammy	

Both are acceptable answers.

Which answer showed more thought and used more interesting language? A or B?

Answer B has many more details and shows a more thorough understanding. Notice the simile in Answer B: "Opening the bottle and reading the message inside was as thrilling as opening presents on my birthday." See the Appendix pages on Figurative Language for added ideas on how to make your writing more interesting.

MORE ABOUT INTERESTING, INSIGHTFUL CONNECTIONS

Showing insight means you use your own words and build on the details from the story. It is your personal stamp on your answer.

The task below has 2 answers attached. Both answers are acceptable. One answer shows more insight. Which answer shows the most interesting, insightful details?

Question: Compare Helena and Sammy; tell how they are alike and how they are different. Use details from the article.	
Answer **A:** Sammy and Helena are two friends who met in a very unusual way. Helena sent a message in a bottle and Sammy found it. Sammy was a nine-year-old boy, and Helena was an eleven-year-old girl. They both live near a beach.	The answer is acceptable. Does it show insight or thought? Is it interesting?
Answer **B:** Sammy and Helena are alike, but they are also different. Sammy is a boy, and Helena is a girl. Sammy is nine, and Helena is eleven. They both live near a beach.	The answer is acceptable. Does it show insight or thought? Is it interesting?

Both are acceptable answers.

Which answer showed more thought and used more interesting language? A or B?

Answer choice A is more detailed and complete.

C IS FOR CONCLUDING SENTENCE, ORGANIZATION THAT'S CLEAR, CORRECT SPELLING, GRAMMAR, AND PUNCTUATION

Concluding Sentence

DO

- highlight the main ideas
- provide an ending

DO NOT

- use the same language as in the introduction
- end too simply with no reference or connection to the main idea
- use "in conclusion…"

Clear Organization

- Your writing is easy to understand.
- You are able to make your point.

Correct

Spelling—Look back in the reading selection and the task. Some words you need to write may have been spelled for you in the task. Please see Chapter 4 (pages 100–104) for a list of commonly misspelled words.

Grammar—Pay attention to how you use words in sentences and sentences in paragraphs. Most of the time you will need to write in complete sentences on the ELA test.

Punctuation—Please see Chapter 4 for common rules for punctuation.

You be the teacher. Choose the best concluding sentence for each response.

Sample Response

I am very curious about your island. I am writing this letter to request more information about the island of Grand Turk.

Which is the best concluding sentence?

A That is all.

B I would appreciate any information you could send to help me learn more about your beautiful island.

C In conclusion, I am writing for more information.

The best concluding sentence is B; it includes related details. Choice **A** is *not* detailed, and choice C begins with "in conclusion."

Sample Response

Grand Turk is an island located southeast of Florida and northeast of Cuba in the Atlantic Ocean. The weather here is warm and sunny. There are many beautiful beaches for sunbathing and swimming.

Which is the best concluding sentence?

A I love going to the beach with my family.

B That is all I learned about Grand Turk.

C Its location and weather make it a wonderful place to visit in the middle of winter.

Why do you think choice C is the best concluding sentence?

Return to some of your answers on the previous pages. Check them for conclusion and clear organization. Correct any spelling, grammar, and punctuation errors.

UNDERSTANDING INFORMATION FROM TWO SELECTIONS

Directions: In this section, you are going to read 2 articles. One article is titled "Earth Matters" and the other is titled "Kids to the Rescue." You will complete 2 graphic organizers and write about what you have read. You may look at the articles as often as you like.

Earth Matters

Every year, Americans throw away about 50 billion food and drink cans. They dispose of 27 billion glass bottles and jars. Most of it is taken to a dump, also known as a landfill. It can take from 100 to 400 years for some garbage to decompose, after it is covered with dirt. Glass has been found in perfect condition after being buried for 4,000 years.

Communities are running out of places to bury our garbage. It is time to practice the three R's of the environment: reduce, reuse, and recycle. Everyone can buy less, use less, and reuse things. Using a glass cup instead of a paper one each time we take a drink may save thousands of paper cups. We should also recycle as much as possible. To recycle, we need to separate items so that they can be used again to make new things. Paper, plastic, and glass are all materials that can be recycled.

People of all ages can make a difference. We all need to make less garbage and encourage others to do the same. If we follow the three R's, we won't be down in the dumps anymore.

According to the article, there are ways to solve the garbage problem. Write your answers in the boxes below.

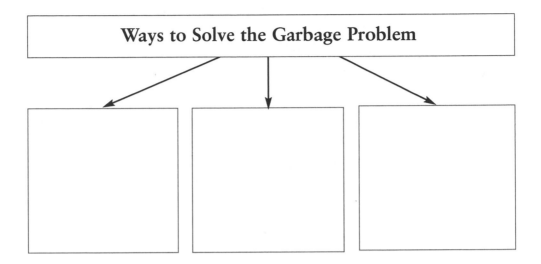

Ways to Solve the Garbage Problem

COMPLETING A GRAPHIC ORGANIZER

Are the boxes below filled in correctly?

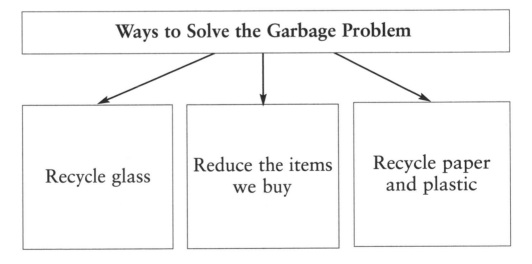

Ways to Solve the Garbage Problem

Recycle glass

Reduce the items we buy

Recycle paper and plastic

The first and last box are similar. The boxes need to have 3 different answers.

Are the boxes below filled in correctly?

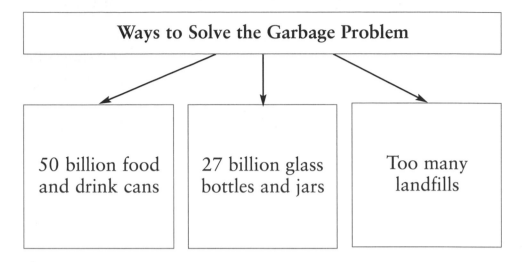

Ways to Solve the Garbage Problem

| 50 billion food and drink cans | 27 billion glass bottles and jars | Too many landfills |

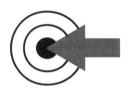

All of these items are problems, not ways to solve problems. None of the answers are correct.

Are the boxes below filled in correctly?

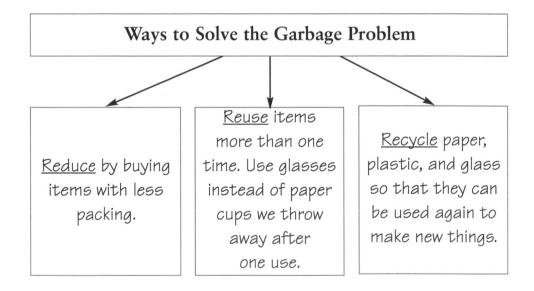

Ways to Solve the Garbage Problem

| <u>Reduce</u> by buying items with less packing. | <u>Reuse</u> items more than one time. Use glasses instead of paper cups we throw away after one use. | <u>Recycle</u> paper, plastic, and glass so that they can be used again to make new things. |

These answers are excellent. They are more detailed and come directly from the reading.

Acceptable Answers = Less Credit or Less Points Earned

- Reduce
- Reuse
- Recycle

Exceptional Answers = More Credit or More Points Earned

- Reduce by buying items with less packaging.
- Reuse items instead of using things and throwing them away.
- Recycle by separating paper, plastic, and glass so that they can be made into something new.

NOT ACCEPTABLE ANSWERS:

- Problems stated, not solutions
- Same answer repeated in more than one box

Kids to the Rescue

environment: our surroundings

Taking care of our environment is an important job, and it's not just a job for grown-ups. There is something for everyone, including children, to do. Some things you can do on your own, some with a friend, and others with the help of an adult. Just look around your neighborhood or school, and think about ways to improve the environment. It is never too late to begin. Here are a few ideas to help you get started.

Keep America Beautiful: Never litter. If your parents own a car, make litter bags for them. Keep your yard free of trash. If your school playground doesn't have a garbage can, ask the principal or custodian to put one out. You can make posters reminding other students to put garbage where it belongs. You can also make a bulletin board showing pictures of clean areas and other areas spoiled by litter or trash.

Kids can make a difference by "reducing," "reusing," and "recycling," often referred to as the 3 R's. They need to educate themselves and others about ways to promote the 3 R's. Environmental clubs encourage groups of children to work together to protect our planet. Some clubs sponsor school-wide environmental education programs and events. Others organize clean-up days in the community and at school.

Directions: Complete the graphic organizer below using information from the article "Kids to the Rescue."

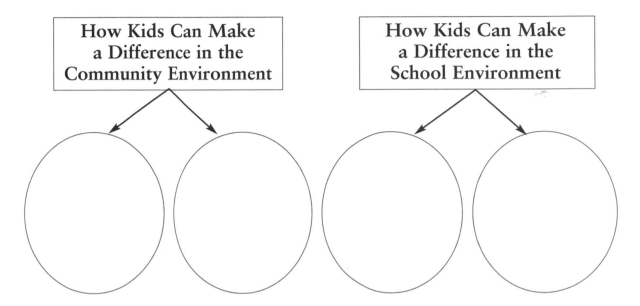

Directions: Look at the graphic organizer below. According to the article "Kids to the Rescue," which item is <u>not</u> correct?

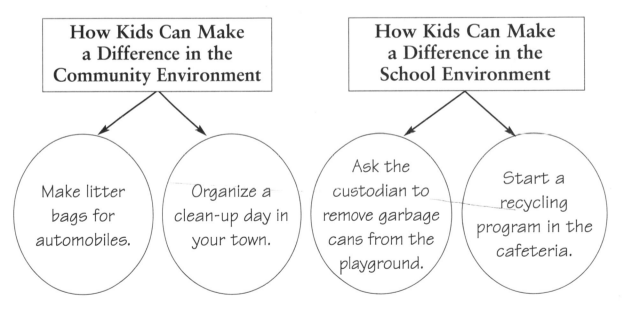

All items are correct except for "ask the custodian to remove garbage cans from the playground." The article suggests that a garbage can should be on the playground.
Information needs to come from the article.

WRITING TO INFORM

The article "Earth Matters" discusses the growing garbage problem our world is facing. What is the main problem with garbage and what are some possible solutions? The article "Kids to the Rescue" shares many ways children can help take care of our environment. Why do you think it is important for students in your school to care about this issue and join the environment club?

Use details from both articles to write an article for the school newsletter encouraging your fellow students to become involved in caring for the environment.

In your answer, be sure to include

- Why garbage is a problem

- Some possible solutions to the garbage problem

- Why students should care about the problem

- Why students should join the environment club

Title: _____

_____

_____

_____

_____

_____

_____

_____

Remember to look for clues in the task or question. In the task below, the underlined words indicate:

Type of writing—ARTICLE

Purpose—INFORM

Audience—COMMUNITY

Source of Information—BOTH ARTICLES

You are a member of your school's environmental club. You need to write an article for the school newsletter informing the community about all the ways you are helping your school.
Use details from both articles to help you write the article.

Sample Response One

Did you know that Americans throw away about 50 billion food and drink cans every year? They are taken to the dump to be covered by dirt. It may take a long time for some things to decompose. Glass can be found in perfect condition after being buried for 4,000 years. Soon communities will run out of places to bury their garbage. As a community we need to reduce, reuse, and recycle. Every person can make a difference.

This answer does not inform the community about ways your club is helping your school. It uses information from just one article. Most items are copied from the article and not written in the author's own words. **The task directions have not been followed.**

Sample Response Two

The Environmental Rangers at Work

Did you know that Americans throw away 50 billion cans and 27 billion glass bottles every year? Students at Hillside Elementary School became concerned when we learned this disturbing fact. We have started a club called the Environmental Rangers. So far, we have organized a recycling program in our cafeteria. Student volunteers separate items such as glass and plastic, which can be used again to make new items. Club members have made posters and bulletin boards to remind other students about the importance of taking care of our environment. The Environmental Rangers are children who are making a difference.

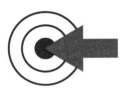

This is an informative response that uses details from both articles. **This answer is acceptable.** An outstanding answer would include even more detail. How did your response measure up?

You are a member of your school's environmental club. You need to write an article for the school newsletter encouraging your fellow students to join the club to help the school.

Use details from both articles to help you write the article.

Title: _____

_____

_____

_____

_____

_____

_____

_____

_____

_____

_____

_____

You are a member of your school's environmental club. You task is to **write an article** for the school newsletter **encouraging your fellow students** to **join the club** to help the school.

   Use details from both articles to help you write the article.

Sample Response One

   The school's environmental club needs your help. Student members do many things around the school. We could do more if we had more members. If you would like to join our club, come to the next meeting. You need to bring only a smile, ideas for helping our school, and plenty of energy to do a very important job. Even Paul Revere, a hero of the American Revolution, recycled. He melted down and reused old silver. You can join our club and recycle, too!

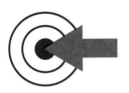

This response does <u>not</u> answer the question. It does not contain information from the articles read. It includes a recycling fact about Paul Revere based on the writer's memory. **Be sure to use information from the articles, even if the topic is familiar to you.**

Sample Response Two

   Caring, Creative Students Wanted

   The environmental club, known as Planet Protectors, needs creative people like YOU who care about our school environment. If you would like to make a difference and help keep our school beautiful, please join our important club.

   Members of Planet Protectors get to do many interesting projects. We help with the school recycling program in the cafeteria, and create bulletin boards to teach students about littering. In the spring, we will be organizing a school clean-up program.

Our club needs your talents and energy. Please come to our next meeting, which will be held tomorrow at 4:00 P.M. in Ms. Wizard's science room. Delicious ice cream sundaes will be served in glass, not plastic, bowls. You will have an exciting time meeting new people and working together to improve our school.

This answer is acceptable. It uses information from both articles and completes the task given. It also includes a title.

HELPFUL TIPS

WORDS YOU SHOULD KNOW

Below you will find a list of important words, their meanings, and some examples. You may already know some of them. The words are used throughout this book and are important for understanding the language and tasks of the ELA. Reviewing the list below will also help you in your language arts classroom.

adjective—describes a noun or pronoun by telling what kind, how many, or which one

Examples: large, empty, kind, smooth, six, some, these, that

Use adjectives in your writing to paint clearer descriptions and details for your readers: "Like *multicolored* paints on a *white* sheet of *drawing* paper, adjectives can turn a *colorless*, *lifeless* piece of writing into a *delightful* work of art."

alliteration—repeating the beginning or middle sounds in words

Example: Try to write stories that have *b*rilliant *b*eginnings, *m*arvelous *m*iddles, and *e*xcellent *e*ndings.

Alliteration is a tool often used by poets to help create the beautiful sounds of language and to make readers remember the words.

antonyms—words with opposite meanings

Examples: happy/sad and big/little

article—a piece of writing, usually about one topic and usually nonfiction

captions—words found next to a picture or illustration that help explain it

character(s)—the people and animals in a story
   Pay attention to:

- the names of characters
- what they look like
- what they say, do, think, and feel
- how characters react to each other.

Note: Pay special attention to how character(s) grow and change.

climax—the most exciting and interesting part of a story
   Readers wonder what will happen next.

compare—to show how persons or things are alike and how they are different

concluding sentence—a reworded topic sentence
   It restates the main idea of the paragraph in different words.

conflict—the problem in the story
   Every story has a conflict.
   The conflict leads to all the action and keeps the reader interested in the story.

contrast—to show how persons or things are different

dialogue—the talking that takes place between characters in a story

essay—a short piece of nonfiction work, which supports a main idea with details and examples

event—a specific action or happening in a selection

fact—a thing known to be true
Example: The beaver is the state animal of New York.

fiction—writing that is made up or invented
Examples: fantasies, adventure stories, mysteries, science fiction, historical fiction

figurative language—words used out of their usual meaning to create a special effect, such as in poetry
It is made up of words that do not mean what they first seem to mean.
Example: "Michelle wrote so much that she wore her fingers to the bone." The sentence is trying to state in an imaginary way that Michelle wrote for a long period of time. It does not mean that Michelle actually wore her fingers to the bone. Figurative language, then, is a special use of words. It is descriptive language that helps readers form a word picture in their minds.

figures of speech—the different ways to use figurative language
Examples: simile, metaphor, personification, and hyperbole
Good writers use figures of speech to create strong word pictures.
When used correctly, figures of speech can greatly improve your writing.
Use figures of speech in your writing, but do not overuse them.
Look for figures of speech in your reading. Pay attention to how writers use figures of speech.

genre—a kind or type of book form
Examples: historical fiction, picture book, fantasy, folktale, biography

graphic organizer—something that organizes information and helps readers understand information at a glance
Examples: chart, diagram, web, story map, picture

homophone—a word that sounds like another word with a different meaning and spelling
  Examples: their, there, and they're

hyperbole—saying more than is true to create an effect; exaggerating or stretching the truth
  Example: Uncle Johnny has so many pennies that instead of saving them in a jar, he stores them in a wheelbarrow.

literal language—language that means exactly what it seems to mean
  Example: "Marilyn wrote for one hour." The words are used in their usual meaning, without stretching the truth.

metaphor—figure of speech that compares two unlike things
  A metaphor often uses some form of the verb "to be" (is, are, was, were) to compare and link the different things
  Example: She is a cuddly bear.

mood—the feelings readers get from a story or picture
  Examples: fear, sadness, danger

moral—the lesson an author is trying to teach, usually in a fable or tale

nonfiction—written material about true people, places, and events

noun—the name of a person, place, thing, or idea
  Examples: boy, woman, tent, hat, happiness

opinion—what a person thinks, believes, or feels
  Example: New York is the best state in the country.

paragraph—a group of sentences that work together to create a main idea
The topic, or opening, sentence states the main idea.
The main (middle) part of the paragraph contains the details that support the topic sentence.
The closing or concluding sentence restates the main idea in a new and different way.
A paragraph usually begins on a new line that is indented.

passage—a piece or section of a written work

personification—giving *human* qualities to things
Example: The building invited me in with open arms.

plot—the action in a story or play; how the order of events in a story or play is arranged
A plot usually involves conflict.

point of view—a position from which angle the story is being told (who is telling the story)

pronoun—part of speech used in place of a noun
Examples: I, you, he, she, him, her, we, they, them, someone, mine

purpose—the reason that the author is writing the piece
Some possible reasons for writing are to describe or explain something, to convince someone to do something, or to tell a story.

resolution—the end of the main problem; the solution

selection—a short piece of writing such as a story or article

sensory details—details that come to us through the senses: sight, sound, smell, taste, touch

Sensory details help readers see, hear, smell, taste, and feel what the writer's describing.

Examples:

- the vivid colors of the leaves (sight)
- the rush of the wind and crunching of the leaves (sound)
- the fresh smell of springtime flowers (smell)
- the taste of berries Mother picked (taste)
- the branches brushing against my arms and leaves (touch)

sequence of events—the order in which things happened

Example: *First* Steven played basketball, *then* he went swimming.

setting—when and where the events of a story happen

Settings can help create the mood of a story.

Stories can be set in the past (history), present (now), or the future (tomorrow).

A setting can be as simple as an afternoon in the park, or as detailed as a year in the busy life of the president.

simile—figure of speech that compares two unlike things using the words "like" or "as"

Examples:

Monica and her best friend, Christina, belong together like popcorn and butter.

Mark jumped up and down like an excited kangaroo when I invited him on our family trip to the mountains.

Ryan's hands are as warm as towels that have just come out of the dryer.

stanza—an arrangement of lines in a poem

story—a written work, either true or made up, which tells the order of events in the lives of characters
A story has a beginning, middle, and end.
A story has a conflict, or problem, to be solved.

story elements—important details about stories
Examples: genre, title, characters, setting, mood, theme, point of view, plot, conflict, climax, and resolution

supporting details—the details (reasons, examples, facts, sensory descriptions) that help writers make a point or develop their stories

synonyms—words that have almost the same meanings
Example: Giant and huge are synonyms for big.
Our language is rich in words. Synonyms can improve your writing because they give you more words to choose from and more ways to say exactly what you mean.

theme—the main idea or meaning in a piece of writing

topic sentence—an opening sentence that gives the main idea of a paragraph

transitions—words and phrases that are like "bridges"; they help connect thoughts and ideas, making it easier for readers to understand a writing piece
Examples: first, then, next, later, before, after, during

verb—a word that shows action or connects two ideas in a sentence
Examples: Mary *sings* and *dances* whenever she *hears* music.
J.J. *is* always helpful.

UNDERSTANDING GENRES

NONFICTION

	Features of Genre	Strategies for Success
Informational Article from a Magazine or Newspaper	Gives factual information about a topic. Organizes facts in a way that helps readers learn about the topic. Photos, illustrations, graphs, charts, and/or diagrams may be used to help support the text. Headings tell about each section in the article.	Underline important text while reading. Read captions carefully: information given in captions is important. Pay attention to the extra information provided by graphic organizers. Note how the information is organized into sections because it helps the reader's search for details. Note the Five W's and One H: who, what, where, when, why, and how.
Editorial	Article is written to express an opinion about a news topic. Article tries to persuade others to agree. Evidence (proof) is given to support the opinion and to defend against other people's arguments.	Think about why the author has written the article and what the author wants readers to believe after reading it. Make connections between the information given; compare and contrast the information being presented.
Interview	An interview with a real person gives factual information about the person's experience.	Pay attention to the questions asked and answers given. Think about the point of view of the person being interviewed.

	Features of Genre	Strategies for Success
Biography	It is the factual story of a person's life, written by someone else.	Pay attention to the events that have shaped the person's life. Chart the person's life in a time line. Note how the person grows and changes over time.

FICTION

	Features of Genre	Strategies for Success
Mystery	The plot includes a problem or puzzle to be solved. Clues are given to keep the reader in suspense. The mood is filled with suspense, danger, and excitement.	Use clues or hints given by the writer to gather details, solve the puzzle, and discover "who done it" (whodunit). Note the use of suspense to hold the reader's attention.
Realistic Fiction	Characters are fictional, but the story is based on situations that could really happen. The setting is a place that readers know or can recognize. Story elements are all present.	Chart the story elements: title, setting, character(s), conflict, events leading to resolution.
Historical Fiction	Setting is a time and place in the past (in history). Some of the characters and events are from history; some are created (made up) by the author.	Compare/contrast the factual (facts) and fictional parts in the story.

	Features of Genre	Strategies for Success
Fable Fables, myths, legends, and folktales began as storytelling and were later written down.	A short tale that usually teaches a lesson or moral. Characters are often animals or non-living things which talk and act like human beings.	Look for animals that act like humans. Note the story elements, the lesson or moral learned, and how the lesson was learned.
Myth Myths and legends often explain how and why things happened in nature.	A myth is a fantasy; it is not based on facts in history. Myths include heroes and heroines who perform amazing acts. Animals in myths play important roles. Often, in myths, good is rewarded and evil is punished.	Note the story elements. Pay attention to the communication between the characters and notice if the myth deals with the ideas of "right" and "wrong."
Legend	Legends may have some truth to them, but they also include made-up material (the truth has been stretched, or exaggerated).	Chart the story elements.
Folktale	Plot is of first importance. Often the lesson to be learned is that good wins over evil. Folktales are different from fairy tales: folktales deal with ordinary people, but fairy tales deal with imaginary beings with magical powers. A tall tale is one type of folktale.	Pay close attention to the plot and to the lesson learned.

	Features of Genre	Strategies for Success
Fantasy	The story could never really happen. Usually the characters and the setting are made up (imaginary), such as other worlds with wizards and dragons.	Pay special attention to the following 3 story elements: setting, characters, and time.
Science Fiction	The main events might really happen, but they are not likely to happen.	Look for the use of time travel, animals that talk, or imaginary beings from other planets.
Adventure Stories	Action-packed tales are filled with suspense and daring characters. Characters, especially the main character, face larger-than-life situations; they need to take risks to solve a problem.	Pay attention to the exciting action and events that make up the plot. Look for brave heroes and mean characters (villains). Note the risks taken for a successful solution to the problem.

POETRY

Poetry	Usually, poems are made up of few words, but there is much meaning packed in the words. Poetry shows the beauty of language: words are often used in a musical way. Poetry shows the power of language: word pictures are often used in a powerful way to describe the mood and the author's experiences and feelings. Poems do not have to rhyme, but often have a rhythm.	Reread the poem: think about the feelings, thoughts, and experiences the poet is trying to describe. Note the use of figures of speech such as personification, similes, and metaphors.

CHARACTER TRAITS: ADJECTIVES FOR PEOPLE

adventurous

brave
bright

calm
careless
cheerful
clever
confused
cooperative
courageous
cowardly
creative
cruel
curious

daring
determined
disagreeable

energetic

fearful
forgetful
forgiving
friendly
fun-loving
funny

generous
gentle
gloomy
greedy

handsome
hard-working
helpful
honest
humorous

imaginative
intelligent

jolly
joyful

kind

lazy
loud
loveable
loyal

messy
mischievous

nagging
neat

obedient
organized

patient
patriotic
playful
pleasant
pleasing
polite
poor
popular
pretty
proud

quarrelsome
quiet

relaxed
respectful
responsible
rich
rude

selfish
sensitive
short
shy
smart
sneaky
stingy
strong
stubborn
studious
successful

talkative
tall
thoughtful
timid
trusting

unfriendly
unkind
unselfish

wise

FREQUENTLY FOUND WORDS

a
about
after
again
all
always
an
and
any
are
around
as
ask
at
ate
away

be
because
been
before
best
better
big
black
blue
both
bring
brown
but
by

call
came
can
carry

clean
cold
come
could
cut

did
does
done
don't
draw
drink

eight
every

fall
far
fast
find
first
five
fly
for
found
four
from
full
funny

gave
get
give
go
goes
going
good
got

green
grow

had
has
have
he
help
her
here
him
his
hold
hot
how
hurt

I
if
in
into
is
it
its

jump
just

keep
kind

laugh
let
light
like
little
live
long
look

made
make
many
may
me
much
must
my
myself

never
new
no
not
now

of
off
old
on
once
one
only
open
or
our
out
own

play
pick
please
pretty
pull
put

ran
read
red
ride
right
round
run

said
saw
say
see
she
sing
sit
six
sleep
small
so
some
soon
start
stop

take
tell
thank
that
the
their
them
then
there
these
they
think
this
those
three
to

today
together
too
try
two

under
up
upon
us
use

very

walk
want
warm
was
wash
we
well
went
were
what
when
where
which
white
who
why
will
wish
with
work
would
write

yellow
yes
you
your

SAMPLE LISTENING/WRITING RUBRIC

Quality	Excellent	Good
Meaning: The extent to which the answer shows understanding and interpretation of the task	-fulfill all or most of the requirements of tasks -address the theme or key elements of text -show an insightful interpretation of text -make connections beyond text	-fulfill some requirements of the tasks -address many key elements of the text -show literal interpretation -make some connections
Development: The extent to which ideas are elaborated, using specific and relevant details and examples	-develop ideas fully with thorough elaboration -make effective use of relevant and accurate examples from the text	-may be brief, with little elaboration, development sufficient to answer question -use relevant and accurate examples to support ideas -may include minor inaccuracies
Organization: The extent to which the response shows direction, shape, and coherence	-establish and maintain a clear focus -shows a logical, coherent sequence of ideas through the use of appropriate transitions	-is generally focused but may include some irrelevant details -show logical sequence of ideas

Developing	Beginning
-fulfill some requirements of the task	-fulfill few requirements of the task
-address basic elements of text, make some weak connections	-miss basic elements of text
-show some understanding of text	-show evidence that the student understood only parts of the text
	-make few if any connections
-may begin to answer the questions, but are not fully developed	-may include a few accurate details
-give some examples and details	
-may attempt to establish a focus	-may focus on minor details or lack focus
-show a clear attempt at organization	-show little or no organization
-may include some irrelevant details	

Quality	Excellent	Good
Language Use: The extent to which the answer shows an awareness of audience and purpose through effective use of words, sentence structure, and sentence variety	-is fluent and easy to read, with vivid language -style is sophisticated, using challenging vocabulary	-writing is fluent and easy to read, with vivid language -using some sentence variety and challenging vocabulary
Conventions: The extent to which the answer shows conventional spelling, punctuation, paragraphing, capitalization, grammar, and usage	The writing shows control of the conventions.	There are few, if any, errors and none that interfere with comprehension. Grammar, capitalization, punctuation, and paragraphing are correct. Misspellings are minor or repetitive.

Developing	Beginning
-is mostly readable, with some sense of engagement -primarily uses simple sentences	-is often repetitive, with little sense of voice -uses minimal vocabulary
The writing shows partial control of the conventions. There are errors that may interfere somewhat with readability but do not interfere with comprehension.	The writing shows minimal control of the conventions. There may be many errors that interfere with readability and comprehension.

COMMONLY MISSPELLED AND CONFUSED WORDS

accept = to receive or to agree with

> I **accept** your apology.

except = other than

> Everyone **except** Sam went swimming.

all ready = completely ready

> We're **all ready** to go camping.

already = tells when

> I have **already** finished my homework.

all right = correct

> **all right is always two words**

> Her answers were **all right**.

a lot = many

> **a lot is always two words**

> I have **a lot** of baseball cards.

Note: Try not to use the word "a lot" in your writing;
Use synonyms such as "several" and "many."

> I have **several** baseball cards.

> I have **many** baseball cards.

all together = people and things in one place at one time

> Our class must stay **all together** on this field trip.

altogether = completely

> I am **altogether** tired.

does = performs (a duty, job, or task)

> She always **does** a splendid job.

dose = amount of medicine

> She needs a **dose** of cough medicine.

hear = what you do with your ears

> Can you **hear** me?

here = a nearby place

> Please put the keys **here**.

hole = an opening through something

> I have a **hole** in my shirt.

whole = complete or entire

> Please do not eat the **whole** bag of popcorn.

hour = time

> We will eat dinner in one **hour**.

our = belonging to us

> **Our** house has high ceilings.

it's = a contraction for it is

> **It's** a beautiful day.

its = belonging to it

> The adorable puppy wagged **its** tail.

knew = the past tense of the verb know

> Jerry **knew** the answer.

new = the opposite of old

> Ellen has a **new** baseball bat.

loose = free, unfastened

> My tooth feels **loose**.

lose = to be unable to find something

> Did you **lose** your backpack?

meat = food

> Carnivores, not herbivores, eat **meat**.

meet = to come upon

> It is a pleasure to **meet** you.

passed = to move beyond

> I **passed** an apple tree on my way to school.

past = a time gone by

> In historical fiction, the setting is a time and place of the **past**.

peace = freedom from fighting and war

> Martin Luther King, Jr., dreamed of world **peace**.

piece = a part of something

> I would enjoy a **piece** of pepperoni pizza.

principal = person in charge of a school *or* the most important part

> A **principal** is like the mother or father of a school. A **principal** is our *pal*.

> My **principal** (main) complaint is that children cannot roller-blade in Seagull Park.

principle = idea

> The Statue of Liberty is founded on the **principle** of freedom.

quiet = making very little noise

>During a fire drill, our class is as **quiet** as an ant in the library.

quit = to stop

>Please **quit** leaving your toys on the floor.

quite = completely

>She is **quite** a talented singer.

than = shows a comparison

>Pamela enjoys playing the flute more **than** anyone in her family.

then = tells when

>**Then** she ran around the track five times.

their = belonging to them

>**Their** favorite sport is soccer.

there = points out a location (place)

>The soccer ball is over **there**.

they're = contraction for they are

>**They're** playing soccer now.

threw = tossed

>Molly **threw** the baseball like a major league pitcher.

through = in one side and out the other

>The refrigerator could not fit **through** the door.

to = in the direction of (toward)

> I went to the store to buy a skateboard.

too = also or too much (very)

> Jack bought a skateboard too.

> The red skateboard is too expensive.

two = the number 2

> Theresa purchased two skateboards.

weather = what it's doing outside

> The weather is delightful.

whether = a choice

> Whether or not I will go depends upon the weather.

who's = contraction for who is

> Who's knocking at the door?

whose = belonging to whom

> Whose lunch box is this?

wood = what trees are made of

> I needed wood to build a doghouse.

would = part of the verb will

> If I had candy, I would share it with you.

you're = contraction for you are

> You're a math wizard.

your = belonging to you

> Your bedroom looks like a toy store.

SYNONYMS FOR OVERUSED WORDS

Instead of using	Try this word	Or this	Now you try
said	exclaimed	screamed	
	muttered	whispered	
good	wonderful	splendid	
bad	terrible	awful	
great	fantastic	excellent	
nice	pleasant	agreeable	
happy	delighted	pleased	
sad	heavyhearted	blue	
like	enjoy	appreciate	
hate	dislike	despise	
big	huge	enormous	
small	petite	tiny	
fast	rapidly	swift	
slow	gradual	unhurried	
fun	amusing	entertaining	
walk	march	stroll	
quiet	hushed	still	
loud	noisy	booming	
scary	creepy	frightening	
look	stare	glance	
tall	towering	lofty	
very	extremely	truly	
kid	youngster	child	
funny	comical	amusing	

ADJECTIVES

Adjectives are describing words that tell what kind, how many, or which one. They make your writing more colorful and give readers a clearer picture of what you're describing.

amazing	lazy	rainy
	long	rare
beautiful		red
black	magnificent	round
blue	many	
bright	mean	sad
	mighty	scary
clever	mushy	short
		silly
dull	nasty	splendid
	new	stingy
fabulous	nutritious	strange
friendly		striped
funny	odd	
	orange	tall
gigantic	ordinary	tender
gorgeous	outstanding	tough
green		tricky
grumpy	precious	
	pretty	ugly
handsome	purple	
horrible		vast
huge	quaint	
humorous	quick	wonderful
	quickest	
jolly	quiet	
kind		

"PEOPLE" WORDS YOU SHOULD BE ABLE TO READ AND SPELL

actor	dancer	king	queen
actress	dentist		
Americans	director	lawyer	relative
artist	doctor	leader	reporter
astronaut		librarian	
athlete	editor	lifeguard	salesperson
aunt	electrician		scientist
author	engineer	mail carrier	seamstress
		manager	secretary
baby	family	mechanic	senator
baby-sitter	farmer	mother	singer
baker	father		sister
banker	firefighter	neighbor	student
boss	friend	nephew	
bride		niece	tailor
brother	gardener	nurse	teacher
builder	grandchild		tutor
bus driver	grandparent	operator	
	groom	owner	uncle
caretaker	guard		
carpenter	guide	painter	waiter
character		parent	waitress
chauffeur	hairdresser	person	wife
chef	hero	people	
child	heroine	photographer	
children	husband	plumber	
citizen		poet	
classmate	infant	police officer	
clown	illustrator	politician	
coach	inventor	president	
conductor		prince	
cousin	judge	princess	
crossing guard			

"GREAT OUTDOORS" WORDS YOU SHOULD BE ABLE TO READ AND SPELL

airplane
American flag
animals
ant
automobile

backpacking
barbecue
baseball
basketball hoop
bay
beach
bee
bicycle
birdbath
blanket
boots
branch
breeze
bridge
bus
butterfly

campsite
canoeing
carnival
caterpillar
chipmunk
clothesline
clouds
compass
cool breeze
curb

daisy
deck
deer
doghouse
driveway

environment

farm stand
field
fire hydrant
flower
football
forest
fresh air

garden hose
gardening
gloves
grass

hiking
hill
hopscotch
horse
hot dog stand

ice-cream truck
ice skating
icicles
insects

jogging
jumping rope

kite

lake
lampposts
lawn mower
leaves
lemonade
lemonade stand
lily
lounge chair

map
mail box
mittens
moonlight
mosquito
mountains

nature
neighborhood

ocean
outdoor concert
outdoor truck

pail
parade
park bench
path
patio
pebbles
picket fence
pinecone
planet
plant
playground
pollen

pond
pool

rabbit
raccoon
rain
rake
recreation
river
road
rocks
rose
running

sailboat
sandbox
scuba diving
seaweed
scarf
scooter
shells
shovel
sidewalk
skateboard

skiing
sky
sledding
snow
soccer
sports
sprinkler
squirrel
stadium
star
stream
street
street lights
summer
summer camp
sun
sunglasses
suntan
surroundings
swan
swimming

telephone pole
temperature

tennis
tent
trail
train
tree
tree house
truck
tulip
twigs

umbrella

valley

walking
wild berries
wildlife
wind
wind chimes
woods
worm

yard sale

SAMPLE WRITING RUBRIC

Quality	3 points
Meaning: The extent to which the answer shows understanding and interpretation of the task	-fulfill the requirements of task -demonstrate insight and make connections
Development: The extent to which ideas are elaborated, using specific and relevant details and examples	-develop ideas fully with elaboration -use relevant and accurate examples to support ideas
Organization: The extent to which the answer exhibits direction, shape, and coherence	-establish and maintain clear focus -show logical sequence of ideas
Language Use: The extent to which the answer shows an awareness of audience and purpose through effective use of words, sentence structure, and sentence variety	-writing is fluent and easy to read, with vivid language -using varied sentence structure and challenging vocabulary
Conventions: The extent to which the answer shows conventional spelling, punctuation, paragraphing, capitalization, grammar, and usage	The writing demonstrates control of the conventions of written English. There are few, if any, errors and none that interfere with comprehension. Grammar, capitalization, punctuation, and paragraphing are correct. Misspellings are minor or repetitive; they occur primarily when a student takes risks with sophisticated vocabulary.

0 = The responses are completely irrelevant or incoherent

2 points	1 point
-fulfill some requirements of the task -make some connections	-fulfill few requirements of the task -make few connections
-may be brief, with little elaboration -provide some examples and details	-may contain a few examples or details
-are generally focused, may contain irrelevant details -show a clear attempt at organization	-may focus on minor details or lack focus -show little or no organization
-are readable, with some sense of engagement -primarily uses simple sentences	-are often repetitive, with little sense of voice -uses minimal vocabulary
The writing demonstrates partial control of the conventions of written English. It contains errors that may interfere somewhat with readability but do not interfere with comprehension.	The writing demonstrates minimal control of the conventions. There may be many errors that interfere with readability and comprehension.

TRANSITION WORDS

Transition words help organize your writing. They are the words that connect thoughts and ideas. The chart below gives three examples for each purpose.

Purpose	Example	Example	Example
To add or show sequence	first	next	last
To show likeness: show how things are alike	also	in the same way	similarly
To contrast: show differences	however	yet	but
To show cause and effect	because	as a result	due to
To give examples	for example	such as	for instance
To show time	now	soon	later
To show place or direction	nearby	far	above
To summarize or conclude	therefore	thus	so

PUNCTUATION TIPS

Ending a Sentence

Period   I think it is a splendid idea.

Question mark   Do you like the idea?

Exclamation mark   I love the idea!

Commas

In dates   February 2, 2004

In addresses   222 Main Street, Hometown, New York

Items in a series   Plants need water, light, and soil to live.

With introductory information   Yes, that is a fabulous idea.

Quotation Marks

Direct quotations—Ms. Hoops said, "Let's continue to work."

Capitalization

Proper Nouns—Proper nouns name a specific person, place, thing, or event

Example: Robert visited the White House on Tuesday, January first. After leaving Washington, D.C., he went to see the Empire State Building in New York City.

First word in sentences and quotations

Titles of works (books, articles, poems, stories)

FIGURATIVE LANGUAGE: SIMILE, METAPHOR, HYPERBOLE, AND PERSONIFICATION

Simile: A simile compares two unlike things using the words "like" or "as." Writers use similes to paint a strong, clear picture in the reader's mind.

Literal Language	Figurative Language: Simile
Joey is tall.	Joey is as tall as the Empire State Building on stilts.
The audience watched me perform on stage.	When I was performing on stage, the audience paid such close attention to me that I felt like an insect being observed under a magnifying glass.
Dayna is pretty.	Dayna is as beautiful as a sunset.

Metaphor: A metaphor compares two unlike things without using the words "like" or "as." It often uses some form of the verb "to be" (is, are, was, were) to compare and link the unlike things. Like similes, metaphors make it easier and more enjoyable for readers to form pictures in their minds.

Literal Language	Figurative Language: Metaphor
Mrs. Lapinski dances gracefully.	Mrs. Lapinski is a ballerina.
Jean's hair feels soft.	Jean's hair is silk.
Transition words and phrases connect ideas.	Transition words and phrases are bridges that connect ideas.

Hyperbole: A hyperbole is an exaggeration. It stretches the truth to create a special effect for the reader.

Literal Language	Figurative Language: Hyperbole
Uncle Victor has a lot of energy.	Uncle Victor is so full of energy that he can recharge a dead battery just by touching it.
Rocco swims many laps in his pool.	Rocco swims so many laps in his pool that the chlorine tablets get seasick from all the motion.
Ms. Oliverio's students pay close attention to their reading material.	Ms. Oliverio's students can get so "lost in a book" that even the police and FBI can't find them.
Elinore's house is very clean.	Elinore's home is so clean that the one tiny speck of dust living there is lonely.

Personification: Personification gives human qualities to nonhuman things.

Literal Language	Figurative Language: Personification
The ice-cream cone fell on the floor.	The ice-cream cone cried vanilla tears when it fell on the floor.
Bruce's muscles are in good shape.	Bruce's muscles sing and dance to celebrate their fine health.

ONLINE RESOURCES

Graphic Organizers

http://www.graphic.org/goindex.html

Language Arts Site

http://www.english-zone.com/

Aesop Fables

www.AesopFables.com

Many fables to hear online

New York State Education Department—Assessment Information

http://www.emsc.nysed.gov/ciai/ela.html

Go to the English Language Arts page for sample tests.

PRACTICE TESTS

PRACTICE TEST 1

DAY 1, SESSION 1—MULTIPLE CHOICE

28 Questions
45 minutes

Directions: In this part of the test, you are going to do some reading and then answer questions about what you have read.

You will be filling in the answers to Numbers 1 through 28 on the answer (bubble) sheet. If you make a mistake, erase it completely. Do not write answers on the test pages. All of your answers must be marked on the answer sheet. You may make notes or underline in the book as you read. Do not use highlighters.

You will have 45 minutes to read all of the selections carefully and answer the 28 questions about what you have read. On the answer sheet, you will fill in the letter that matches your answer for each question.

Try to answer all questions. Read each question carefully, and make your best attempt at answering the question.

SESSION 1—ANSWER SHEET

1. Ⓐ Ⓑ Ⓒ Ⓓ   15. Ⓐ Ⓑ Ⓒ Ⓓ

2. Ⓕ Ⓖ Ⓗ Ⓙ   16. Ⓕ Ⓖ Ⓗ Ⓙ

3. Ⓐ Ⓑ Ⓒ Ⓓ   17. Ⓐ Ⓑ Ⓒ Ⓓ

4. Ⓕ Ⓖ Ⓗ Ⓙ   18. Ⓕ Ⓖ Ⓗ Ⓙ

5. Ⓐ Ⓑ Ⓒ Ⓓ   19. Ⓐ Ⓑ Ⓒ Ⓓ

6. Ⓕ Ⓖ Ⓗ Ⓙ   20. Ⓕ Ⓖ Ⓗ Ⓙ

7. Ⓐ Ⓑ Ⓒ Ⓓ   21. Ⓐ Ⓑ Ⓒ Ⓓ

8. Ⓕ Ⓖ Ⓗ Ⓙ   22. Ⓕ Ⓖ Ⓗ Ⓙ

9. Ⓐ Ⓑ Ⓒ Ⓓ   23. Ⓐ Ⓑ Ⓒ Ⓓ

10. Ⓕ Ⓖ Ⓗ Ⓙ   24. Ⓕ Ⓖ Ⓗ Ⓙ

11. Ⓐ Ⓑ Ⓒ Ⓓ   25. Ⓐ Ⓑ Ⓒ Ⓓ

12. Ⓕ Ⓖ Ⓗ Ⓙ   26. Ⓕ Ⓖ Ⓗ Ⓙ

13. Ⓐ Ⓑ Ⓒ Ⓓ   27. Ⓐ Ⓑ Ⓒ Ⓓ

14. Ⓕ Ⓖ Ⓗ Ⓙ   28. Ⓕ Ⓖ Ⓗ Ⓙ

Directions: Read this poem about autumn. Then answer questions 1 through 5.

Autumn Fancies

Anonymous

The maple is a dainty maid,
The pet of all the wood,
Who lights the dusky forest glade
With scarlet cloak and hood.

pet: favorite

dusky: dark

The elm a lovely lady is,
In shimmering robes of gold,
That catch the sunlight when she moves,
And glisten, fold on fold.

The sumac is a gypsy queen,
Who flaunts in crimson dressed,
And wild along the roadside runs,
Red blossoms in her breast.

crimson: red

And towering high above the wood,
All in his purple cloak,
A monarch in his splendor is
The proud and princely oak.

monarch: king

1. In the poem "Autumn Fancies," the trees are described as

   A animals

   B insects

   C people

   D towers

2. The tallest of all the trees in the forest is the

   F elm

   G oak

   H sumac

   J maple

3. How does the maple affect the woods?

   A it lights up a dull forest

   B it is the favorite

   C it towers over all of the other trees

   D it acts like a queen

4. Of all of the trees mentioned, which one would probably not be chosen to be planted in someone's yard?

   F maple

   G oak

   H elm

   J sumac

5. When the author of the poem describes the maple as the "dainty maid," he or she means that the maple is

   A wild

   B lovely

   C small

   D tall

Directions: Read this article about a famous monument. Then answer questions 6 through 10.

A Proud Lady in the Harbor

Who wears a crown with seven huge spikes, has an index finger longer than the height of a very tall basketball player, and wears a size 879 in women's shoes? The answer, of course, is the world-famous Statue of Liberty. It was the first site that immigrants saw when they arrived in America.

In 1884 France gave the Statue to the United States as a symbol of the friendship these two countries had made during the American Revolution. The huge copper structure was shipped to the United States in 1885 in 214 cases. Over the years, the monument has also come to symbolize freedom under America's free form of government.

The Statue, whose proper name is "Liberty Enlightening the World," stands proudly 115 feet above New York Harbor. It is a tremendous sculpture of a lady, who is dressed in a loose robe. She holds a torch in her right hand, which is raised high in the air. Her left arm holds a tablet containing the date of the Declaration of Independence: July 4th, 1776. People hardly notice the broken shackles underfoot, which represent Liberty destroying the chains of slavery. The seven spikes in her crown stand for either the seven seas or the seven continents.

Millions of people visit the Statue annually. Many visitors climb 354 steps to reach the crown, which contains 25 windows. The normal waiting time to climb to the crown in the summer is three hours. Some visitors take an elevator to the base of the statue, where there is an observation balcony and view of the city. The original torch, which was replaced when the structure was restored in the 1980s, is now at the base.

Today, next to the flag of the United States, the Statue is America's most common symbol for freedom.

tablet: book

shackles: chains

restored: repaired

6. What is the main idea of this article?

   F   Lady Liberty has a large foot and index finger.

   G   Visitors can either climb many stairs or take the elevator to view different parts of the monument.

   H   The Statue of Liberty is a well-known monument and symbol for freedom.

   J   Visitors to the Statue of Liberty should take more time and notice the important broken shackles by her feet.

7. The spikes on the crown of the Statue of Liberty look most like

   A   the seven continents

   B   the rays of the sun

   C   the seas

   D   windows

8. Which of the following is an *opinion* from the article?

   F   France gave the monument to the United States in 1885.

   G   The Statue of Liberty holds a torch in her right hand.

   H   It was kind of France to give the United States the Statue of Liberty.

   J   There are 25 windows in Lady Liberty's crown.

9. According to the article, millions of people visit the Statue of Liberty annually. What does the word "annually" mean?

   A monthly

   B weekly

   C yearly

   D every two years

10. What is the most likely reason that the Statue was shipped to the United States in 214 cases?

   F The height of the Statue is 214 feet.

   G The cases stood for the 214 battles in the American Revolution.

   H The Statue was very large and had to be taken apart before being shipped.

   J It took 214 long, hard days to build the monument.

Directions: Read the article about animals' tails. Then answer questions 11 through 15.

A Tail Comes in Handy

Animals use their tails for different purposes. You can learn fascinating information about animals just from observing their tails.

A tail comes in handy for communication. Animals such as wolves and ostrich use their tails to show rank among the group. A timid wolf will keep its tail between its legs, whereas a fearless wolf will raise its tail. The highest-ranking male ostrich will hold his tail pointing straight up to show his dominance. The next-highest male will hold his tail horizontal, while other birds droop their tails down to show they are subordinate.

communication: talking

subordinate: lower in rank

Deer also use their tails to communicate with each other. A white-tailed deer will lift its tail straight up and wag it, showing the white fur underneath. The white fur acts like an alarm or signal, which warns other deer of approaching danger.

A tail comes in handy for balance purposes. The kangaroo and the squirrel use their tails for balance. A kangaroo's tail acts like a third leg; it allows the animal to prop itself up. The squirrel's bushy tail not only provides warmth on winter days, but it also helps the animal keep its balance when it is leaping and climbing.

A tail comes in handy for movement. Birds use their tails to move around and balance on branches. Most fish have tails that help them with movement and direction.

A tail comes in handy to scare off predators. Many animals use their tails to give a warning that they feel threatened and are ready to defend themselves. To warn would-be attackers, a rattlesnake will rattle its tail and a porcupine will raise its quills and shake them. A ground iguana scares off its enemies by whipping its tail fiercely. Horses, giraffes, cows, and lions have tails that can swat off the peskiest of flies.

Tails serve many purposes. They can be as useful to animals as a baseball is to a pitcher.

11. According to the definition given in the article, which of the following words is the <u>opposite</u> of *subordinate*?

   A junior

   B higher

   C lesser

   D inferior

12. The main idea of the article is that

   F tails can help protect against predators

   G animals use their tails in many ways

   H some animals could not survive without tails

   J tails come in many shapes and sizes

13. The article suggests that animals use their tails for protection in all of the following ways <u>except</u>

   A warning others to stay away

   B warning before striking

   C warning with smell

   D warning others in the group of approaching danger

14. The word *timid* means

   F powerful

   G brave

   H shy

   J silly

15. Which word from below should be used to complete both blanks in the graphic organizer?

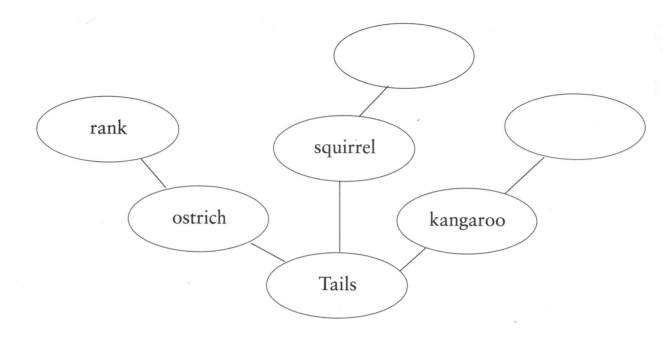

A warmth

B signal

C communicate

D balance

Directions: Read the poem entitled "The Kayak." Then answer questions 16 through 19.

The Kayak

Anonymous

Over the briny wave I go,
In spite of the weather, in spite of the snow:
What cares the hardy Eskimo?
In my little skiff, with paddle and lance,
I glide where the foaming billows dance.

Round me the sea-birds slip and soar;
Like me, they love the ocean's roar.
Sometimes a floating iceberg gleams
Above me with its melting streams;
Sometimes a rushing wave will fall
Down on my skiff and cover it all.

But what care I for a wave's attack?
With my paddle I right my little kayak,
And then its weight I speedily trim,
And over the water away I skim.

skiff: small boat

16. What word would best describe the water being traveled?

   F calm

   G smooth

   H glassy

   J rough

17. How does the kayaker feel about the ocean?

   A he loves it

   B he is afraid of it

   C he hates it

   D he is troubled by it

18. What does the kayaker not see in his travels?

   F snow

   G birds

   H icebergs

   J waterfalls

19. The phrase "foaming billows dance" describes

   A birds flying around

   B Eskimos dancing

   C water bubbling strongly

   D kayak bouncing around

Directions: Read the tale below. Then answer questions 20 through 24.

The Stone in the Road
Adapted Tale

This story took place long ago in the kingdom of a very wise king, who was always attempting to teach people good habits. He often tested others to see if they were thoughtful, good people. He believed that people should do less complaining and solve their own problems.

One night, while everyone slept, he placed a large stone in the road that led past his palace. He hid at the edge of the road to see what would happen.

A short time afterward, a soldier marched casually along the road. The soldier's foot struck the rock, and he sprawled in the road. The soldier rose angrily, waving his sword at the rock. He complained to himself as he continued down the road, blaming lazy people for leaving the rock in the road; never once did the soldier think that he should move the stone himself.

After a few more minutes, a farmer guided his grain wagon around the rock in the road. He was on his way to the mill to have his grain ground to flour, and he did not have time to stop and remove the rock.

"The world is filled with careless, lazy people!" the farmer complained. "Someone should remove the rock from the road so that it doesn't cause an accident."

All day long the king secretly watched people go around the rock and complain about lazy people leaving the rock in the road: yet no one touched the rock to move it.

It was almost evening when a young girl walked past the palace. She was very tired from working at the mill all day. She spotted the rock and thought, "I should move this rock from the road; it is almost dark and someone may trip and get hurt."

She struggled with the heavy rock and managed to move it aside. Beneath the rock was a box. She lifted the heavy box out of the hole it was in. On it was written, "This box belongs to the thoughtful one who moves the stone out of the way for others."

The girl opened the box and discovered it was filled with gold. The news of her find spread throughout the area. The soldier and the farmer and the other passersby went back to the spot in the road to search in the dust for a piece of gold.

The king announced the find: "As we go through life, we often are faced with obstacles and problems. We may complain while we just walk around them waiting for someone else to solve them, or we can take the time to solve the problems ourselves. If we leave problems for someone else to solve, we are usually disappointed."

20. Why did the king bury the gold under the rock?

    F to teach people a lesson

    G to hide it from people

    H to save the gold

    J to keep it safe

21. The farmer did not move the rock because

    A he was in a hurry

    B he drove around it

    C he didn't notice it

    D he thought someone else should take care of it

22. What was the soldier most likely thinking when he passed the rock in the road?

    F it was a trick

    G it was left by the farmer

    H it was left by a lazy person

    J he should move the rock

23. When she saw the stone in the road, the young girl

    A walked around it

    B complained about the careless person who had left it there

    C moved it before someone was hurt

    D went to the king for help

24. What lesson was the king probably trying to teach?

    F everyone has a duty to make changes for the good of all

    G people are careless and leave things lying around

    H sometimes when you least expect it, good things happen

    J you should always watch where you are going

Directions: Read the article about roller coasters. Then answer questions 25 through 28.

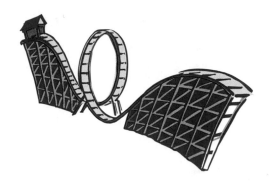

Roller Coasters: Scream Machines

When you think of roller coasters, you probably imagine amusement parks on summer days. If so, your mental picture is very different from their origins in fifteenth-century Russia in the cold of winter.

The first roller coasters earned the nickname "Russian Mountains." They were ice-covered hills, constructed of wood. Children and adults would climb up five stories of stairs (70 feet high) and sit on an ice block for the 50-mile-per-hour ride that would last just a few seconds.

In 1804, the ride "Russian Mountains" was brought to Paris, France. Wheels were added to the sleds. Little was done to make the ride safe, which seemed to attract more riders. It took a number of years for safety measures to be improved.

In 1827, a coal mining company in Pennsylvania opened "Gravity Road" (a converted railway that rolled downhill to transport coal) to the public for amusement purposes. This would be one of the first roller coasters in the United States. Many of the next roller coasters were built in amusement parks on Coney Island in New York. This increased competition led to new, more daring innovations and the required safety improvements.

Today, the roller coaster with the biggest drop is located in California. It is called the "Super Man Escape" and has a drop of 328 feet. The fastest coaster is in Japan; it reaches speeds of 107 miles per hour. The ride of the future will undoubtedly be taller and faster.

25. The author wrote this article to

   A persuade people to ride roller coasters

   B increase the safety of roller coasters

   C learn about all the different roller coasters today

   D review the history of roller coasters

26. According to the article, what happened as roller coasters became more daring?

   F fewer people rode

   G they were made more comfortable

   H safety improvements were needed

   J height and weight restrictions were important

27. One of the first roller coasters in the United States was

   A located on Coney Island

   B made of ice

   C in an amusement park

   D used to transport coal

28. Which is <u>not</u> a nickname for roller coasters?

   F Scream Machines

   G Paris Mountains

   H Russian Mountains

   J Gravity Road

DAY 2, SESSION 2—LISTENING

2 short answers
1 long response
45 minutes

Directions: In this section of the test, a story called "Doing What Comes Naturally" will be read aloud to you twice. Please listen carefully each time the story is read because you will then be asked to answer specific questions about the story.

During the first reading, listen closely but do not take notes. You may take notes during the second reading. Please use the space provided below for your notes. You may refer back to your notes to answer the questions that follow. Your notes will *not* count toward your score.

Notes

Doing What Comes Naturally

An African Tale

Long ago in an African jungle, Monkey and Rabbit were enjoying a meal together. Rabbit was enjoying his bounty of green leaves, and Monkey was dining on bunches of yellow bananas.

During the feast each acted naturally. Rabbit turned his head, first to the left, then to the right, then behind him, and finally in front of him. He was always watching for an enemy. He was not able to stop looking around, even during the meal.

As Rabbit was on the lookout, Monkey scratched. He scratched all over: his arms, legs, chest, and head. He was unable to stop the scratching. Rabbit watched and asked, "Did you sit on an ant's nest? Something is making you scratch."

"I didn't sit on an ant's nest; I scratch naturally," responded Monkey firmly.

"Please stop; it is very impolite," demanded Rabbit.

"You should talk about being impolite; you have been looking around the whole time we have been eating," answered Monkey.

"I will stop looking around, if you stop scratching," replied Rabbit.

"I think I can stop for longer than you can," boasted Monkey.

"The first one to move has to feed the winner for a week," announced Rabbit.

They continued their lunch, with no scratching or looking around. Thirty minutes passed. Monkey wanted to scratch himself more than a person who had a bad case of the chicken pox. And Rabbit was shaking with fear.

Rabbit suggested that the two tell each other stories while they ate. He began: "One night, my mother left me to watch over my brothers and sisters. I was frightened by every sound. I heard a twig snap to my left and then to my right...." Rabbit acted out the story looking to the left and

then to the right. "Then I heard something in the trees above," Rabbit stated as he looked up.

Monkey laughed, realizing that Rabbit was trying to trick him. He began his story, "One day I was separated from my mother in the jungle; I was hit on the head with a branch." Monkey scratched his head. He continued, "Then I discovered a nest of bees and was stung on my chest over and over again." He took the opportunity to scratch his chest repeatedly.

Rabbit stopped Monkey's story; "I guess we can't change what comes naturally to us."

Monkey agreed. "I think you are right."

Today, Rabbit and Monkey continue to eat their meal, looking around and scratching happily.

29. Complete the story chart with details from the tale.

```
┌─────────────────────────────────────────┐
│ Beginning of the story                  │
│                                         │
│                                         │
│                                         │
└─────────────────────────────────────────┘

┌─────────────────────────────────────────┐
│ Middle of the story                     │
│                                         │
│                                         │
│                                         │
└─────────────────────────────────────────┘

┌─────────────────────────────────────────┐
│ End of the story                        │
│                                         │
│                                         │
│                                         │
└─────────────────────────────────────────┘
```

30. This story is titled, "Doing What Comes Naturally." What would be another title for the African tale? Use details from the tale to support your answer.

_____

_____

_____

_____

_____

_____

31. This African folktale teaches a lesson. Which lesson does the folktale teach best? Use details from the tale to support your answer.

■ Love your neighbors for who they are.
■ Be yourself; don't try to be something you're not.

_____

_____

_____

_____

_____

_____

_____

_____

_____

_____

_____

_____

DAY 3, SESSION 3—READING AND WRITING

60 minutes
Read 2 selections.
Write one short answer based on the first selection.
Write 2 short answers based on the second selection.
Write a long response based on both selections.

Directions: In this section of the test, you will read a web site called the "Aunt Tillie's Web Site of Alaska," and an e-mail from a class of fourth-grade students from Alaska. Then you will answer some questions and write about what you have read. You may look back at the web site and e-mail as often as you like to help you answer the questions.

AUNT TILLIE'S WEB SITE OF ALASKA

Browse This Educational Site and Learn the Fun Facts About This Fantastic State from an Expert on Alaska: Aunt Tillie

The name Alaska means "great land" or "that which the sea breaks against."

• **Capital City is Juneau**
• **Largest City is Anchorage**
• **Bordering U.S. States—None**
• **Bordering Country—Canada**

Alaska became our 49th state on January 3, 1959.

Fun Facts About Alaska

• On October 18, 1867, the United States purchased Alaska from Russia for 7.2 million dollars.
• In 1880, there was a gold rush.
• Alaska is the largest state in the United States. It is over twice the size of Texas. The state of Rhode Island could fit into Alaska more than 400 times.
• Most of America's salmon and crab come from Alaska.
• The most important source of income (money) for Alaska is the oil and natural gas industry.

Mountains Everywhere

• 39 mountain ranges
• 17 of the 20 highest peaks in the United States are located in Alaska
• Mount McKinley, in Alaska, is the highest point in North America

FLAG: In 1926, a 13-year-old Native American boy named Benny Benson designed the official Alaskan flag. His flag contained eight gold stars on a blue field. The blue field is for the sky and the wild forget-me-not, the state flower. The star in the upper right stands for the North Star, representing Alaska's northern location. The seven stars stand for the Big Dipper, representing strength.

Alaska's Weather Changes from Year to Year

Following are averages only:

• Average January temperatures range from 8 to 21 degrees
• Average February temperatures 26 degrees
• Average July temperatures range from 51 to 65 degrees
• Annual precipitation is 15.9 inches
• Annual snowfall is 69–71 inches

Official State Symbols

• **flower:** the wild forget-me-not
• **bird:** willow ptarmigan
• **tree:** sitka spruce
• **state mineral:** gold
• **insect:** four-spot skimmer dragonfly
• **fish:** giant king salmon

32. Use Aunt Tillie's web site to complete the boxes below. Your answer must include

- one fact about mountains in Alaska
- one fact about the Alaskan flag
- one fact about Alaskan state symbols

Include facts from the web site only.

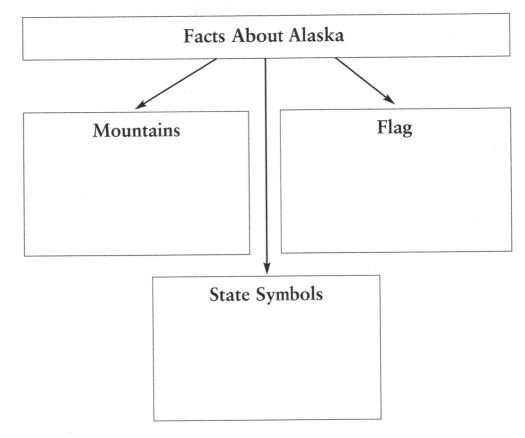

Below is an e-mail sent by Mr. Peabody's fourth-grade students from Anchorage, Alaska. They are interested in becoming e-pals (pen pals corresponding by e-mail) with fourth-grade students in another part of the United States.

To: Fourth Grade Students in New York
From: Fourth Grade Students in Alaska

Re: We Want to be e-pals

Hello e-pals,

We are interested in becoming e-pals with fourth-grade students. Our class would like to learn about life as a fourth grader in another part of the United States.

When you think of Alaska, you probably think of igloos and sledding. The truth is, however, that most Alaskans live in modern houses. Many of us also own and drive cars. Sledding is no longer the main transportation in our northern state.

Alaskans like to participate in outdoor activities including dogmushing, skiing, snowmobiling, canoeing, backpacking, rock climbing, and biking. Dogmushing, or sled dog racing, is the state sport of Alaska. Today, people come to Alaska from all over the world to see the Iditarod Race from Anchorage to Nome. This famous sled dog race lasts for about nine days. Mushers and their loyal, strong, heavily coated dogs race along frozen rivers and icy tundra.

Alaska is sometimes called the "Land of the Midnight Sun." This is because in the summer, it is light outside until almost 11:00 P.M. The sun appears to circle in the sky rather than set. In some of the villages in the northernmost parts of Alaska, the sun doesn't set for 84 days!

We hope you have learned some interesting facts about Alaska.

Please write back soon!

Your Northern Friends

33. Use information from the e-mail to complete the web with dogmushing facts.

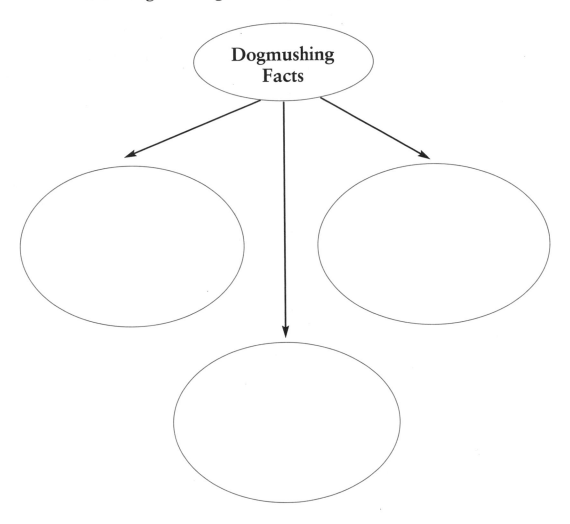

34. Write an e-mail in response to the e-mail sent by the fourth-grade students in Alaska. In your e-mail, be sure to

- include at least 3 interesting details about New York State
- ask questions about the information presented by the Alaskan students in their e-mail, so that you can learn more about life in Alaska

To: Fourth-Grade Students in Alaska
From: Fourth-Grade Students in New York State

Re: Eager to be e-pals

_____
_____
_____
_____
_____
_____
_____
_____
_____
_____
_____
_____
_____
_____

35. Your teacher has encouraged your class to become
e-pals with students from another state. You have
received many e-mails from around the country. You
have decided that you would like to correspond with
students in Alaska. It is your job to write a speech to
present to your classmates to convince them to vote
for writing to Alaskan e-pals. Be sure to use information from both the web site and the e-mail.

_____

_____

_____

_____

_____

_____

_____

_____

_____

_____

_____

PRACTICE TEST 2

28 Questions
45 minutes

Directions: In this part of the test, you are going to do some reading and then answer questions about what you have read.

You will be filling in the answers to Numbers 1 through 28 on the answer (bubble) sheet. If you make a mistake, erase it completely.

Do not write answers on the test pages. All of your answers must be marked on the answer sheet. You may make notes or underline in the book as you read. Do not use highlighters.

You will have 45 minutes to read all of the selections carefully and answer the 28 questions about what you have read. On the answer sheet, you will fill in the letter that matches your answer for each question.

Try to answer all questions. Read each question carefully, and make your best attempt at answering the question.

SESSION 1—ANSWER SHEET

1. Ⓐ Ⓑ Ⓒ Ⓓ   15. Ⓐ Ⓑ Ⓒ Ⓓ

2. Ⓕ Ⓖ Ⓗ Ⓙ   16. Ⓕ Ⓖ Ⓗ Ⓙ

3. Ⓐ Ⓑ Ⓒ Ⓓ   17. Ⓐ Ⓑ Ⓒ Ⓓ

4. Ⓕ Ⓖ Ⓗ Ⓙ   18. Ⓕ Ⓖ Ⓗ Ⓙ

5. Ⓐ Ⓑ Ⓒ Ⓓ   19. Ⓐ Ⓑ Ⓒ Ⓓ

6. Ⓕ Ⓖ Ⓗ Ⓙ   20. Ⓕ Ⓖ Ⓗ Ⓙ

7. Ⓐ Ⓑ Ⓒ Ⓓ   21. Ⓐ Ⓑ Ⓒ Ⓓ

8. Ⓕ Ⓖ Ⓗ Ⓙ   22. Ⓕ Ⓖ Ⓗ Ⓙ

9. Ⓐ Ⓑ Ⓒ Ⓓ   23. Ⓐ Ⓑ Ⓒ Ⓓ

10. Ⓕ Ⓖ Ⓗ Ⓙ   24. Ⓕ Ⓖ Ⓗ Ⓙ

11. Ⓐ Ⓑ Ⓒ Ⓓ   25. Ⓐ Ⓑ Ⓒ Ⓓ

12. Ⓕ Ⓖ Ⓗ Ⓙ   26. Ⓕ Ⓖ Ⓗ Ⓙ

13. Ⓐ Ⓑ Ⓒ Ⓓ   27. Ⓐ Ⓑ Ⓒ Ⓓ

14. Ⓕ Ⓖ Ⓗ Ⓙ   28. Ⓕ Ⓖ Ⓗ Ⓙ

Directions: Read this poem about dandelions. Then answer questions 1 through 5.

Dandelion

Anonymous

There was a pretty dandelion
With lovely, fluffy hair,
That glistened in the sunshine
And in the summer air
But oh! This pretty dandelion
Soon grew old and gray;
And, sad to tell! Her charming hair
Blew many miles away

1. What stage of the dandelion plant is described in the beginning of the poem?

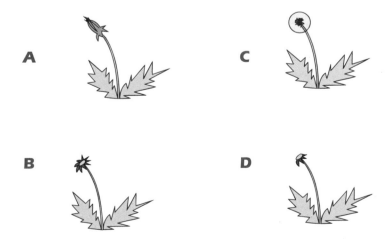

2. The mood in the poem changes from beginning to end;
   it changes from

   F happy to sad

   G sad to happy

   H excited to scared

   J scared to excited

3. What probably caused the hair to be gone?

   A the sun started shining

   B it started raining

   C it was summer

   D a strong wind blew

4. The season described in the poem is

   F winter

   G spring

   H summer

   J fall

5. In the poem, the word "charming" means

   A pleasing

   B fluffy

   C old

   D gray

Directions: Read the following Chinese tale. Then answer questions 6 through 13.

How to Weigh an Elephant
Adapted Chinese Tale

One day a Chinese emperor received an elephant as a gift from a friend. The emperor was amazed by the size of the creature and wanted to know the weight of the elephant. He commanded his advisors to solve this problem. If they could not tell the weight of the elephant in three days, they would be punished.

The advisors had very small scales, much too small to weigh the immense elephant. They were completely stumped by this challenge. On the third day, a young boy came to share his idea with the advisors. They listened doubtfully, but then decided to give the boy a chance to try his weighing method. They went to the river together.

doubtfully: unsure

First, the boy put the elephant in a boat. Then, he swam around the boat and marked the water line with red paint. He removed the elephant and filled the boat with stones until the side of the boat reached the previous water line, marked with red paint. The boy then weighed all of the stones. He now knew the weight of the elephant. The young boy's creative idea worked, which saved the advisors from punishment. And, the emperor was delighted to learn the weight of his gift.

6. Which is the best description of the young boy in the story?

   F lucky

   G kind

   H clever

   J mean

7. What happened right after the emperor received the elephant?

   A he wanted to know the weight of the elephant

   B he was amazed by the size of the elephant

   C he asked his advisors to weigh the elephant

   D a young boy weighed the elephant

8. The word "creature" refers to the

   F boy

   G advisors

   H emperor

   J elephant

9. What will most likely happen the next time the emperor has a problem to solve?

   A he will call the advisors to help

   B he will call the boy to help

   C he will call his friend

   D he will threaten to punish people

10. This story proves that

    F younger people are always smarter than older people

    G elephants are heavy

    H problem solving sometimes requires creativity

    J scales need to be made larger

11. Which word would best describe the emperor?

    A kind

    B demanding

    C clever

    D helpful

12. The meaning of the word "immense" is

    F small

    G very dangerous

    H tiny

    J very large

13. Which of the following events should fill in the box in the timeline?

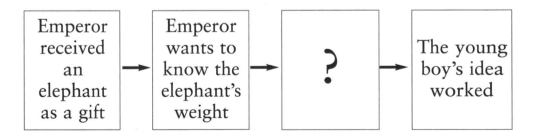

    A Emperor is amazed by the size of the elephant

    B Advisors are not able to weigh the elephant

    C Young boy saves advisors from punishment

    D Emperor was happy to learn the weight

Directions: Read this poem about cobwebs. Then answer questions 14 through 19.

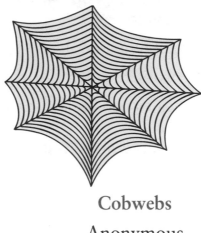

Cobwebs

Anonymous

dainty: delicate

Dainty fairy lace-work, O so finely spun,
Lying on the grasses and shining in the sun,
Guess the fairies washed you and spread you out to dry,
And left you there a-glistening and a' shining to the sky!

14. The cobwebs described in the poem would most likely be found in a

F field

G barn

H basement

J house

15. According to the poem, the cobwebs were created by

A spiders

B the sun

C fairies

D grasses

16. The speaker in the poem uses the word "you" to refer to the

    F reader

    G sun

    H grasses

    J cobwebs

17. The poet uses the phrase "lace-work" to describe the

    A grasses

    B shining sun

    C fairies

    D weaving of cobwebs

18. What may have inspired the poet to write about cobwebs?

    F a dislike of cobwebs

    G a fear of spiders

    H a love of cobwebs

    J a curiosity of fairies

19. The opposite of "dainty" is

    A strong

    B tiny

    C clean

    D small

Directions: Read the article about potato chips. Then answer questions 20 through 24.

The Original Potato Chip

Today, potato chips are a very popular snack. The original chips had a very interesting beginning, in Saratoga Springs, New York, in a restaurant called Moon Lake Lodge.

patron: customer

A famous patron of Moon Lake Lodge ordered a new dish called French fries, which he had first had in Paris, France. The chef at Moon Lake Lodge was not French, but he was able to cook many French dishes. He made the French fries and sent them to the customer. The customer sent the fries back to the kitchen because they were too thick. He insisted he wanted thin fries.

The chef quickly made a batch of thinner French fries. These were still not correct according to the paying guest. The chef became angry and sliced the potatoes so thin that you could almost see through them. He fried them to a crisp, salted them, and served them himself. He was surprised to observe the customer enjoying the chips and was even more surprised to receive a compliment.

version: variety

Before long, potato chips were such a hit that they were added to the restaurant's menu. In 1887, the American version of the French fry, today known as the potato chip, was included in the White House cookbook.

20. The author probably wrote this article to

    F   teach readers about how to make potato chips

    G   persuade readers to eat chips

    H   explore the varieties of potato chips

    J   inform readers about how potato chips were invented accidentally

21. Which of the following words was <u>not</u> used to identify the visitor to the restaurant?

    A   patron

    B   paying guest

    C   customer

    D. mister

22. According to the article, potato chips were first served in

    F   Paris

    G   New York

    H   the White House

    J   France

23. The customer <u>did not</u> like French fries that were too

    A   thick

    B   thin

    C   small

    D   salty

24. The first potato chips were made in an attempt to

    F   advertise a new restaurant

    G   make a chef angry

    H   create a new French recipe

    J   get back at a "picky" customer

Directions: Read the poem about rain. Then answer questions 25 through 28.

The Rain

Anonymous

"Open the window, and let me in,"
    Sputters the merry rain;
"I want to splash down on the carpet, dear,
    And I can't get through the pane."

"Here I've been tapping outside to you,
    Why don't you come, if you're there?
The windows are shut or I'd dash right in,
    And stream down the attic stair."

"I've washed the windows, I've spattered the blinds
    And that is not half what I have done;
I've bounced on the step and the sidewalk too
Till I've made the good people run."

pane: divided window

25. In the poem, the rain is trying to communicate to the

A people on the sidewalk

B windows of the house

C people inside the house

D people who are running

26. Why did the people run?

F they needed to close the windows

G water was splashing onto the carpet

H water was streaming down the stairs

J the rain was splashing on the sidewalk

27. In the poem, the word *dash* means

A tap

B rush

C shut

D step

28. The rain is responsible for

F splashing down on the carpet

G tapping outside

H streaming down the attic stairs

J splashing in the window

DAY 2, SESSION 2—LISTENING

2 short answers
1 long response
45 minutes

Directions: In this section of the test, a story called "How the Ostrich Got His Long Neck" will be read aloud to you twice. Please listen carefully each time the story is read because you will then be asked to answer specific questions about the story.

During the first reading, listen closely but do not take notes. You may take notes during the second reading. Please use the space provided below for your notes. You may refer back to your notes to answer the questions that follow. Your notes will *not* count toward your score.

Notes

How the Ostrich Got His Long Neck
Adapted African Tale

Introduction to the Tale: Long ago, Ostrich had a short neck, like all the other birds. That was . . . until his encounter with Crocodile.

Ostrich wanted to be friends with Crocodile, even though he was warned that it would be a big mistake.

Monkey gave Ostrich this advice, "Don't trust Crocodile; he has no manners and he's mean. His favorite pastime is scaring all of the animals away from the river."

Then Ostrich asked Wildebeest for his opinion and he received this warning, "Crocodile is lazy; he lies around all day waiting for his dinner to walk past."

Elephant also added his own two cents, "Crocodile would not be a good friend; he thinks only of himself. He will snap at you if he gets a chance."

Ostrich decided to ignore the advice of his friends and play with Crocodile.

One day, Crocodile was hungry. He asked Ostrich to look in his mouth to see what was wrong with his tooth. Crocodile opened his jaws very wide. Ostrich wanted to help a friend so he stuck his head inside.

"You have so many teeth," Ostrich announced with amazement. "How will I know which one is aching?"

"It's the one in the back," Crocodile moaned.

So, Ostrich kept sticking his head further and further into Crocodile's mouth.

Crocodile saw his chance and snapped his jaws shut on Ostrich's head.

Ostrich yelled for help, but no one heard because all the other animals stayed as far away from Crocodile as they could. He started to pull. Crocodile pulled back. They both continued to pull. Ostrich's neck began to stretch.

It stretched longer and L-O-N-G-E-R.

Ostrich continued to pull because he did not want to lose his head.

Crocodile grew tired, stopped pulling, and finally let go. Ostrich jumped back away from shore.

To this day, Ostrich has a long neck to remind him to stay away from Crocodile.

29. Complete the boxes below with Crocodile's character traits from the tale.

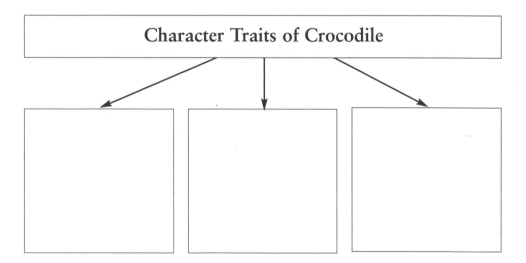

30. In the tale "How the Ostrich Got His Long Neck,"
the statement "Elephant also added his own two
cents" means

_____

_____

_____

_____

_____

_____

_____

_____

_____

_____

_____

_____

31. In the tale "How the Ostrich Got His Long Neck," Ostrich learns a very good lesson. Which lesson below does the tale best teach? Use examples from the tale to support your choice.

- ▪ Listen to your friend's advice.
- ▪ Choosing the wrong friends can be bad for you.

_____

_____

_____

_____

_____

_____

_____

_____

_____

_____

_____

DAY 3, SESSION 3—READING AND WRITING

60 minutes
Read 2 selections.
Write one short answer based on the first selection.
Write 2 short answers based on the second selection.
Write a long response based on both selections.

Directions: In this section of the test, you are going to read 2 selections. Then you will answer qustions about what you have read.

TECHNOLOGY NEWSLETTER

Health Concerns Addressed

Doctors report seeing increasing numbers of children with computer-related injuries.

Back, neck, and wrist injuries are related to the increase in computer use among younger children.

Experts suggest teaching children good posture and proper techniques early to decrease this trend.

Helping Kids Connect

For years, kids have had pen pals. They have used the mail to correspond with their long-distance friends. Today, kids use the Internet to create new friendships and join cooperative projects.

Some classroom exchange programs offer instant translation, making it easier to have a non-English speaking e-pal. Live chats with experts and monitored e-mail accounts have features that overcome the safety concerns.

Contact *Classroom Exchange.net* for more information.

Video Game Club Forming Based on Popular Demand

All students interested in joining the video game club should report to the cafeteria on Thursday after school.

Members will play games and share game strategies. Games containing violence will not be allowed. Look forward to an exciting, social time!

32. According to the newsletter, what are some of the positive and negative effects technology may have on the lives of children? Write your answer in the boxes below.

Positive Effects of Technology on Lives of Children	Negative Effects of Technology on Lives of Children

Fashions for the Twenty-first Century

| functioning: working |

Computer scientists and the clothing makers are working together to produce clothes that are functioning computers. They are called "wearable computers."

Today there are many experimental models being tested. The items range from a hooded jacket with an MP3 player that plays music, to clothes for soldiers that warn of approaching vehicles. One company is working on a sneaker that will tell runners how fast they are moving.

| image: picture |

Other wearable computers are built into eyeglasses. This eyewear allows an image to be projected onto one eye, while the other eye can still see what is in front of it. Doctors are experimenting with this technology to assist them in surgery.

The makers of this wearable clothing admit that it will be some time before some of these items will be available to the public. Fabrics containing the technology need to be more durable; they are still easily damaged.

In the near future, our computers may be wash and wear.

33. What are "wearable computers?" What are some reasons people might be excited about these new inventions? Be sure to use examples from the article.

_____

_____

_____

_____

_____

_____

34. According to the article, why are we not able to buy all of these inventions in the stores today?

_____

_____

_____

_____

_____

35. Technology is everywhere today. It affects almost every part of our life. What are some of the ways that technology influences lives?

Be sure to include examples from both the newsletter on technology and the article on fashions.

_____

_____

_____

_____

_____

_____

_____

_____

_____

_____

_____

_____

PRACTICE TEST 3

28 Questions
45 minutes

Directions: In this part of the test, you are going to do some reading and then answer questions about what you have read.

You will be filling in the answers to Numbers 1 through 28 on the answer (bubble) sheet. If you make a mistake, erase it completely. Do not write answers on the test pages. All of your answers must be marked on the answer sheet. You may make notes or underline in the book as you read. Do not use highlighters.

You will have 45 minutes to read all of the selections carefully and answer the 28 questions about what you have read. On the answer sheet, you will fill in the letter that matches your answer for each question.

Try to answer all questions. Read each question carefully, and make your best attempt at answering the question.

SESSION 1—ANSWER SHEET

1. Ⓐ Ⓑ Ⓒ Ⓓ   15. Ⓐ Ⓑ Ⓒ Ⓓ

2. Ⓕ Ⓖ Ⓗ Ⓙ   16. Ⓕ Ⓖ Ⓗ Ⓙ

3. Ⓐ Ⓑ Ⓒ Ⓓ   17. Ⓐ Ⓑ Ⓒ Ⓓ

4. Ⓕ Ⓖ Ⓗ Ⓙ   18. Ⓕ Ⓖ Ⓗ Ⓙ

5. Ⓐ Ⓑ Ⓒ Ⓓ   19. Ⓐ Ⓑ Ⓒ Ⓓ

6. Ⓕ Ⓖ Ⓗ Ⓙ   20. Ⓕ Ⓖ Ⓗ Ⓙ

7. Ⓐ Ⓑ Ⓒ Ⓓ   21. Ⓐ Ⓑ Ⓒ Ⓓ

8. Ⓕ Ⓖ Ⓗ Ⓙ   22. Ⓕ Ⓖ Ⓗ Ⓙ

9. Ⓐ Ⓑ Ⓒ Ⓓ   23. Ⓐ Ⓑ Ⓒ Ⓓ

10. Ⓕ Ⓖ Ⓗ Ⓙ   24. Ⓕ Ⓖ Ⓗ Ⓙ

11. Ⓐ Ⓑ Ⓒ Ⓓ   25. Ⓐ Ⓑ Ⓒ Ⓓ

12. Ⓕ Ⓖ Ⓗ Ⓙ   26. Ⓕ Ⓖ Ⓗ Ⓙ

13. Ⓐ Ⓑ Ⓒ Ⓓ   27. Ⓐ Ⓑ Ⓒ Ⓓ

14. Ⓕ Ⓖ Ⓗ Ⓙ   28. Ⓕ Ⓖ Ⓗ Ⓙ

Directions: Read this tale about the wind and the sun. Then answer questions 1 through 6.

The Wind and the Sun

An Indian Tale Retold

The North Wind bragged of great strength. The Sun, however, protested this claim and argued that there was power in gentleness. But the North Wind did not understand how something could be both strong and gentle.

"I see a way to end our dispute. We shall have a contest," said the Sun.

At that time a man was traveling along a winding road. He was wearing a warm winter coat.

"As a test of strength," said the Sun, "let us see which of us can take the coat off that man. You begin."

The Sun rested behind a cloud and watched the Wind at work.

"It will be quite simple for me to force the man to remove his coat," boasted the Wind.

The Wind blew and blew. It blew so hard that birds clung to the trees. The world was whirling with dust and leaves. The harder the Wind blew, the tighter the shivering man clung to his coat. The Wind finally ceased and allowed the Sun to try.

The Sun came out from from behind a cloud. It warmed the air and lighted the road for the traveling man. As the road became warm, the man unbuttoned his coat.

The Sun grew brighter and brighter.

Soon the man felt so hot he took his coat off and sat down in a shady spot along the road.

"How did you do that?" said the Wind.

"It was easy," said the Sun, "I lit the day with gentleness."

1. Which word best describes the North Wind?

   A breezy

   B gentle

   C hot

   D boastful

2. What happened right after the Wind started to blow?

   F the Sun went behind a cloud

   G the birds clung to the trees

   H the Sun came out from behind a cloud

   J the man held his coat closed

3. According to the tale, the winner of the contest will be the one that

   A makes the man rest

   B makes the birds fly away

   C makes the road dustier

   D makes the man take his coat off

4. Read this sentence from the story: "How did you do that?" This sentence refers to

   F the Wind wondering how the Sun got the man to take off his coat

   G the Wind asking the Sun how it shines so strongly

   H the Sun wondering how the Wind blows so strongly

   J the Sun wondering how the Wind blows leaves around

5. The author of the tale most like wanted to show that

   A the Wind is always stronger than the Sun

   B the Sun is always weaker than the Wind

   C gentleness is sometimes the best strength

   D being boastful shows strength

6. Read this sentence from the tale: "The Sun, however, protested this claim and argued that there was power in gentleness." This sentence refers to

   F the Sun winning the contest in the end

   G the Wind winning the contest in the end

   H the Sun disagreeing with the Wind about being strong

   J the Wind bragging about strength

Directions: Read this article about spiders. Then answer questions 7 through 12.

The Barn Spider

The barn spider, native to the northeastern United States and Canada, became famous as a lovable character in the novel *Charlotte's Web*. It is called a barn spider because it is found primarily around and in barns. It is also found around houses, caves, and rocky cliffs. The barn spider weaves an orb web that is sometimes called a wheel web because of its round shape.

The most difficult part of making a web is the first thread. Many people think the spider flies, jumps, or shoots the web like the Spiderman character. Instead the spider starts by releasing a sticky thread that is blown in the wind. A breeze catches it and carries one end to a spot where it sticks. This creates a bridge for the spider. The spider then cautiously crosses the thin line while reinforcing the thread as it goes. The spider continues to construct the web strand by strand. When the web is complete with nonsticky spokes on the wheel and sticky, circular threads, then the spider waits.

In the late afternoon and night, the spider waits in the center of the web. Insects fly or crawl on the web and get entangled in the sticky threads. The spider rushes to its prey and wraps it in special silk thread before biting it. After a night of hunting the web becomes worn. The spider will recycle the silk in the morning by eating it and only leaving the first thread. After resting nearby during the day the spider begins to construct a new web. If the web is not heavily damaged from the nighttime catches, then the spider will reuse it after making some minor repairs.

The spider characters created by authors all have special abilities. The barn spider may not be able to write words or shoot its web, but the creation of a regular web is an amazing feat. The next time you see a spider web, take a closer look at the amazing masterpiece created daily by this small creature.

7. Why do you think the author wrote the article about barn spiders?

    A to share information about spiders

    B to share information about spider characters

    C to share a fear of spiders

    D to warn everyone about the dangers of spider webs

8. An orb web is shaped like a

    F barn

    G nest

    H wheel

    J bridge

9. How does the spider web get started?

    A the spider flies from corner to corner

    B the spider jumps to connect the thread

    C the spider shoots the thread from its legs

    D the wind blows the thread

10. Read this sentence from the article: "After a night of hunting the web becomes worn." In this sentence the word "worn" most likely means

  F to put on its body

  G to be damaged

  H to be full

  J to be tired

11. According to the article, the most difficult part of making a web for the barn spider is

  A keeping it repaired

  B making it round

  C making it sticky

  D the first thread

12. The barn spider would not be able to make a web without help from

  F the insects

  G the wind

  H people

  J sticks

Directions: Read this article about piggy banks. Then answer questions 13 through 17.

The History of the Piggy Bank

Who invented the piggy bank? How did a mud-loving animal become the symbol of saving money? In fact, coin banks weren't always made to look like pigs. Long ago the word "pig bank" came from the name of inexpensive mud like clay and not the animal. During the 1500s in Europe metal was very expensive. So, many household items were made from pygg clay including dishes, plates, and jars. Thrifty families often kept extra coins in one of their pygg jars. These containers became commonly known as pygg jars or piggy banks.

Several hundred years later potters began making clay pots in the shape and likeness of a pig, and thus the piggy bank was born. Adults and children fell in love with these new piggy banks, and the trend spread quickly in England and throughout the rest of Europe.

In some European countries it was a tradition to give a piggy bank to both children and adults to bring luck and good fortune. In German-speaking countries craftsmen gave piggy banks to their apprentices to reward them for the years of hard work spent learning their profession. Children in China have been given "lucky pig" banks for centuries, as their parents encouraged saving money. In Holland, children saved money in a pig-shaped box which was not opened until Christmas. This was known as the "feast pig." Even today lucky pigs are exchanged at the start of the new year.

thrifty = not wasteful

trend = style or tradition

Today's banks come in all shapes, sizes, and colors. They are no longer made of pygg clay, but ceramic, glass, gold, silver, wood, pottery, metal, and plastic. Technology has modernized the coin bank; some have moving parts, and others even compute the money added. The most popular design, however, is still the simple piggy bank.

13. The chart below shows the order of events described in the article.

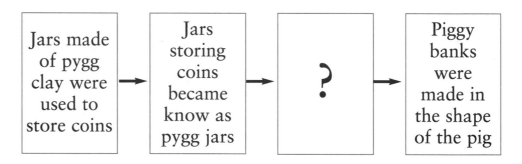

Which event best completes this chart?

A piggy banks are still popular today

B jars and dishes were made of pygg clay

C piggy banks became popular throughout the world

D pygg jars became known as piggy banks

14. Read this sentence from the story. "The piggy bank was born." This sentence refers to

F piggy banks being made of pygg clay

G piggy banks being popular throughout the world

H piggy banks being shaped like a pig for the first time

J piggy banks given to babies when they are born

15. Piggy banks became popular in Europe because

   A people thought they brought them luck

   B people thought they were very expensive

   C people liked gold banks

   D people liked pygg clay

16. The first piggy banks were made of pygg mud because

   F it was inexpensive

   G it was expensive clay

   H they looked like pigs

   J it was lucky

17. Piggy banks were given to children to

   A make them smile

   B encourage saving money

   C reward them

   D create a trend

Directions: Read this article about animals predicting the weather. Then answer questions 18 through 22.

Can Animals Predict the Weather?

In the days before modern technology, meteorologists, and satellite systems, people made observations of the nature around them to forecast the weather. Native Americans, farmers, and sailors depended on these predictions. Many years of observing nature created beliefs about how animals can predict weather. These beliefs have become weather lore. Scientists have recorded and studied some of this lore.

Animals predicting rain is probably the most popular bit of weather lore. Here are some signs that are supposed to mean that rain is on the way. Frogs will croak louder and longer than usual when they sense rain. Dogs whine and act nervous, while cats get very active. Birds fly lower to the ground and gather on tree branches and telephone wires when it is about to rain.

There is weather lore about telling temperature. Crickets are said to be accurate thermometers. They chirp faster when warm and slower when cold. It has been observed that if you count the chirps for fourteen seconds, and then add forty, you will have the temperature of wherever the cricket is.

Several other animal lores are traditional, long-term indicators of the weather. The coat on the woolly bear caterpillar indicates a long, cold winter or a mild winter. If the brown segment between the two black segments is long, then the winter will be mild. In a similar way, squirrels are often used to forecast the coming of winter. If their tails are bushy or they are collecting many nuts in the autumn, then a severe winter should be expected. In the United States a groundhog is used to predict weather six weeks in advance. If a groundhog's shadow is visible at noon on the second day of February, then the weather will be cold and wintry for another six weeks.

People still disagree about the accuracy of weather lore. Some believe they are superstitions or old wives' tales. Others believe they are based on centuries of observation and therefore should not be dismissed.

18. Crickets chirp faster when

    F it gets colder

    G they are nervous

    H the air is warmer

    J it is going to rain

19. What detail from the article is **not** an example of an animal predicting rain?

    A crickets chirping faster

    B frogs croaking louder

    C dogs whining and acting nervous

    D birds flying lower to the ground

20. Read this sentence: "If their tails are bushy or they are collecting many nuts in the autumn, then a severe winter should be expected." The word "severe" means

    F warm

    G prediction

    H harsh

    J natural

21. Before meteorologists and satellite systems how did people forecast the weather?

    A they used modern technology

    B they asked the farmers

    C they asked the sailors

    D they observed the nature around them

22. The word "forecast" most likely means

    F predict

    G observe

    H study

    J consider

Directions: Read this poem about an American symbol. Then answer questions 23 through 28.

An American Symbol

The American Bald Eagle celebrated
and grand,
In 1782, became the symbol of a
new land.

Found from Alaska to the
Florida Coast;
It seemed like the perfect national bird
to most.

Ben Franklin argued the Eagle's
character was lacking;
Thus, another native bird, the turkey,
received his backing.

After years of debate the Bald Eagle was crowned;
Its majestic images are now world renowned.

Flying to speeds of 100 miles per hour and
hunting with keen eyesight,
Eagles leave their diet of fish and other
small prey less than a fair fight.

Bald eagles build enormous 2000-pound nests,
A lofty home for 20 to 30 years, whenever
they need to rest.

Once an endangered species, the population
continues to gain.
Now protected and respected many of them remain.

renowned =
well known

keen = sharp

The Bald Eagle exhibits beauty and
proud independence,
The living symbol of America's freedom,
spirit, and pursuit of excellence.

23. According to the poem, the bald eagle is

    A no longer protected

    B no longer the national bird

    C no longer endangered

    D no longer beautiful

24. The phrase "new land" refers to

    F Florida

    G Alaska

    H the Florida Coast

    J America

25. Ben Fanklin did **not** want the eagle to be the national bird because

    A he knew they were protected

    B he didn't think they had good character

    C he knew they were endangered

    D he knew the eagle was fast

26. Why were the turkey and the eagle the two choices for the national bird?

    F both were native to the United States

    G both were fast

    H both build big nests

    J both were endangered

27. Which of these lines from the poem suggests that pictures of the Bald Eagle are famous?

   A Now protected and respected many of them remain.

   B It seemed like the perfect national bird to most.

   C Its majestic images are now world renowned.

   D The Bald Eagle exhibits beauty and proud independence.

28. Complete the chart below.

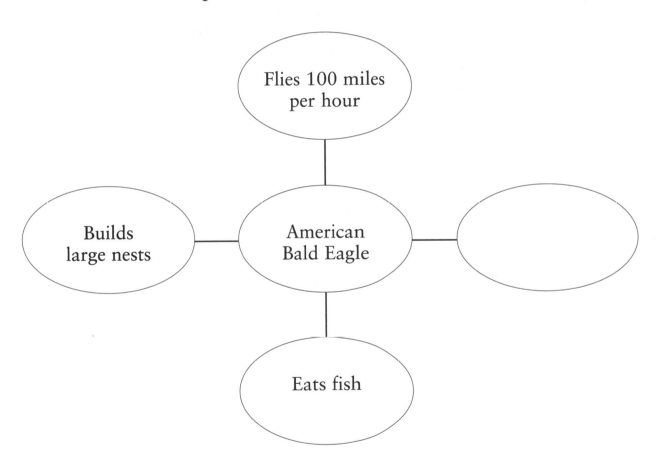

   F likes turkeys

   G more than 300 years old

   H found worldwide

   J has good eyesight

DAY 2, SESSION 2—LISTENING

2 short answers
1 long response
45 minutes

Directions: In this section of the test, a story called "The Whistling Champ" will be read aloud to you twice. Please listen carefully each time the story is read because you will then be asked to answer specific questions about the story.

During the first reading, listen closely but do not take notes. You may take notes during the second reading. Please use the space provided below for your notes. You may refer back to your notes to answer the questions that follow. Your notes will *not* count toward your score.

Notes

The Whistling Champ

The trophy stood tall and proud on Grandfather's very crowded book-shelf. It read, "Whistling Champion 1956." I felt whenever I went into the room that it was there mocking me. My grandfather was a champion whistler. He could chirp and tune, whistle like the birds, and whistle a loud call or warning. He was the best whistler I knew.

My grandfather taught my mom to whistle when she was a little girl. My mother still whistles when she gardens and cooks dinner. She was never a champion, but she loved to whistle. My dad and my little brother could whistle. As a matter of fact everyone in my family could whistle.

Everyone, except me, of course.

I could not whistle a note. My grandfather eagerly instructed me. My mom and dad encouraged me, and my little brother even gave me pointers. I tried and tried, I would pucker up and blow, but, I was still unsuccessful.

I would try to whistle on my walk to the bus stop. I would whistle on my walk home from the bus stop. I would whistle until my best friend told me to stop. I would practice during my chores. I would whistle in the shower. How could someone from a family of whistlers, and a champion no less, not be able to whistle? Every visit I would ask my grandfather for another lesson. He never tired or became frustrated with my lack of ability.

One day while taking the garbage out I puckered up, and sure enough instead of wet air I heard a tone, a tone that sounded like a note. I tried again and heard another note. I whistled and whistled until it hurt to pucker up, and then I whistled some more. I whistled myself to sleep.

The next day, I woke early hoping it had not been a dream. I puckered and cautiously blew. There it was—the beautiful, long-awaited notes. I could not wait for our visit to my grandfather's that day.

I raced into my grandfather's house to demonstrate my chirping skills for him. As I whistled a choppy tune my grandfather's smile grew and grew. When I was finished, he gave me a big hug. He then turned to his bookshelf and removed the trophy. He held it out and said that it now belonged to me. He said, "Emily, that whistling was the sweetest sound I have ever heard."

That night I whistled myself to sleep as the trophy looked on proudly from the shelf in my bedroom.

29. Emily's feelings about the trophy change from the beginning of the story to the end of the story.

Parts of the Story	Feelings About the Trophy
Beginning of the story	
End of the story	

30. Why do you think Emily's grandfather gave her
the championship trophy at the end of the story.
Use examples from the story to support your answer.

_____

_____

_____

_____

_____

_____

_____

_____

_____

_____

_____

_____

31. How do Emily's feelings change from the beginning
to the end of the story? What causes the change?
Use details from the story to support your answer.
Be sure to

- include how Emily feels at the beginning of the story
- describe how Emily feels at the end of the story
- explain what causes the change in her feelings
- use examples from the story to support your answer

_____

_____

_____

_____

_____

_____

_____

_____

_____

_____

_____

DAY 3, SESSION 3—READING AND WRITING

60 minutes
Read 2 selections.
Complete a chart and 1 short answer based on the
    first selection.
Write 1 short answer based on the second selection.
Write an extended response based on both selections.

Directions: In this part of the test you are going to read two articles, "Homing Pigeons" and "Smoke Signals." Then you will answer questions and write about what you have read. You may look back at both articles as often as you like to help you answer the questions.

Directions: Read this article about homing pigeons. Then answer questions 32 and 33.

Homing Pigeons

Visit almost any park in any city and you will see pigeons. These birds like feasting on spilled food under park benches and perching on tree branches. If you think that they are only a nuisance, then you need to learn more about pigeons. Pigeons can fly at speeds of 30 to 40 miles per hour. They also have the ability to find "home" from no matter where they are. In fact, pigeons have been reported to fly over 2000 miles to reach home. Scientists have researched this unique ability and believe that the following are at least three reasons for it.

1. Pigeons seem to be able to tell directions, such as north, south, east, and west by using the sun. Pigeons are born knowing this.
2. Pigeons have a tiny bit of magnetite in their heads. This is the same material that people use in compasses. This material gives the pigeon a built-in compass.
3. Some pigeons seem to be able to smell their way home. They sniff the blowing wind searching for the familiar smells of home.

For thousands of years this homing ability has made the use of pigeons very popular for sending messages. A messenger pigeon would be taken from its cage, and a tiny tube containing a message would be tied to its leg. Roman emperors used pigeons to communicate with faraway lands during a time when riders on horseback would take weeks to cover the same distance. They became the best communication tool in China, Greece, Italy, and India. In the 1800s Julius Reuter founded Reuter's news service, which still exists throughout the world today, 150 years later.

Today there are better ways of communication in most of the world, but some people still use carrier pigeons. For example, a doctor on an island off of France sends blood samples to a lab for testing. The pigeon carries a tube of blood in the pocket of a vest that it wears to do its duty. The blood can be carried to the lab faster by pigeon than by boat, the other available transportation. Pigeons are kept primarily for the sport of racing. Competitors are people who have made raising and training pigeons a hobby. The strongest, fastest pigeons, with the best homing abilities are the winners.

32. Complete the chart below with **three** details from the story to explain the unique homing abilities of pigeons.

Reasons for the Homing Ability of Pigeons
(1)
(2)
(3)

33. Why were pigeons used to help people communicate? How did that method of communication change over time?

_____

_____

_____

_____

_____

_____

_____

_____

_____

_____

_____

_____

Directions: Read the following article about smoke signals. Then answer questions 34 and 35.

Smoke Signals

Human beings have the need to communicate. From the earliest times several methods have been developed in order to share information and to express feelings. There are many different kinds of communication. A simple sound such as a siren or the beat of a drum can communicate a message.

One early form of communication was practiced long ago and is still used at times today. A smoke signal is a visual form of communication used to send signals over a long distance.

This communication was developed in China and in America. Signals were sent by first building a fire. When the fire was covered with a blanket and then quickly removed, a puff of smoke was made. The number, size, and shape of the puffs sends a message to those watching from a long distance. The fires were usually made on very high hills.

Long ago, Native Americans were able to signal trouble or send messages with smoke signals. Even though each of the signals was visible to all, they were not always understood by everyone. Each tribe or group had its own signals, which only their members could interpret. Stone bowls created on mountains and hilltops were the evidence of this widely used communication system.

There were a few standard signals. One puff meant ATTENTION. Two puffs meant ALL'S WELL. Three puffs of smoke signified DANGER, TROUBLE, or CALL FOR HELP.

The Great Wall of China had signaling stations constructed into the towers along the wall. The Chinese used smoke signals to communicate information along the original 6000-mile wall. The smoke signals were combined with gunshots to signal danger from oncoming enemies. It was refined to let other guards even know the number of enemy troops approaching.

Smoke signals are still used today by Boy Scouts. Although modern technology like cell phones make smoke signals unnecessary, they can still be valuable at times. For example, when someone is stranded and has no other way to communicate, then they could build a fire and use smoke signals to call for help.

34. Why were smoke signals used to help people communicate? How did that method of communication change over time?

_____

_____

_____

_____

_____

_____

_____

_____

_____

35. Think about "Carrier Pigeons"and "Smoke Signals."
How are these methods of communication alike?
How are the methods of communication different?
How have both methods of communication changed?
Use details from **both** stories to support your answer.
In your answer, be sure to

- ▪ tell how smoke signals and carrier pigeons are alike
- ▪ tell how smoke signals and carrier pigeons are different
- ▪ tell how both methods of communication change
- ▪ use details from both stories to support your answer
- ▪ check your writing for correct spelling, grammar, capitalization, and punctuation.

_____

_____

_____

_____

_____

_____

_____

_____

_____

ANSWERS AND ANSWER EXPLANATIONS

PRACTICE TEST 1

"Autumn Fancies"

1. **C** The maid, lady, queen, and monarch are words that describe people.

2. **G** In the last stanza, the poet writes that the "oak" is towering high above the wood.

3. **A** According to the first stanza in the poem, the maple lights the dusky forest glade. Dusky was defined as dark.

4. **J** In the third stanza, the poet states that the sumac grows wild along the roadside.

5. **C** The meaning of the word dainty is small.

"The Statue of Liberty"

6. **H** The main idea of the article is that the Statue of Liberty is a famous symbol for freedom. The other letter choices are details about the Statue, but they do not tell the **big** idea of the paragraph.

7. **B** Be careful: This question can be tricky. The spikes on the Statue of Liberty's crown **stand for** either the seven continents or seven seas, but they **look** most like the rays of the sun. The correct answer is choice **B**.

8. **H** A fact is something that can be proven to be true so choices **F**, **G**, and **J** are incorrect because they are facts. An opinion is what someone feels or believes about something: If one thinks it was kind of France to give America the Statue, then that's an opinion. The correct answer is choice **H**.

9. **C** The word "annually" means yearly. A clue to the word's meaning is given in the question: If **millions of** people visit the Statue annually, choices **A** (monthly) and **B** (weekly) would not be likely answers.

10. **H** The huge Statue had to be taken apart before it was shipped. It arrived in America in 214 cases, or crates. The other choices are not supported by information given in the article.

"A Tail Comes in Handy"

11. **B** The opposite of subordinate (lower) is higher.

12. **G** The entire article is about the different ways animals use their tails. Choice **F** is a fact from the article, but it is only a supporting detail (not the main idea). Choices **H** and **J** are not mentioned in the article.

13. **C** The article did not mention that animals use their sense of smell for protection.

14. **H** Read the entire sentence containing the vocabulary word. According to the article, a timid wolf will keep its tail between its legs, whereas a brave wolf will raise its tail. The word timid means shy. The other word choices (powerful, brave, silly) would not make sense.

15. D The word "balance" completes both empty circles because both the kangaroo and squirrel use their tails for balance.

"The Kayak"

16. J The word "rough" matches the descriptions in the poem: "foaming billows," "ocean's roar," and "rushing wave."

17. A Like the sea-birds (second stanza), the kayaker loves the ocean.

18. J The kayaker sees snow, birds, and icebergs; he does not see waterfalls.

19. C The phrase "foaming billows dance" describes the water; choice C is the only choice that describes the water.

"The Stone in the Road"

20. F The king wanted to teach people a lesson.

21. D According to the tale, the farmer thought someone else should take care of the rock.

22. H The soldier thought that the rock was left by a lazy person.

23. C The tale states that the girl moved the stone.

24. F The king felt that people had a duty to solve problems, rather than wait for others to solve them.

"Roller Coasters: Scream Machines"

25. D The article is a review of the history of roller coasters, beginning with their origins in fifteenth-century Russia.

26. H The article states that safety improvements were needed.

27. D One of the first roller coasters in the United States also hauled coal.

28. G The nickname "Paris Mountains" does not appear in the article.

29. Complete the story chart with details from the tale.

Beginning of the story
Rabbit and Monkey were eating a meal. Rabbit kept looking around and Monkey kept scratching.

Middle of the story
The looking around bothered Monkey and the scratching annoyed Rabbit, so each of them tried to get the other to stop the troubling behavior. It was very difficult for them to change and behave in an "unnatural" way.

End of the story
Both of them decided to act naturally, rather than trying to be something that they were not.

30. This story is titled, "Doing What Comes Naturally." What would be another title for the African tale? Use details from the tale to support your answer.

Sample Response

Another interesting title for the African tale would be, "Just Be Yourself." The characters in the tale tried to change each other. Rabbit wanted Monkey to stop scratching himself, and Monkey wanted Rabbit to stop looking around. Both of them learned that they were more content when they were just being themselves, rather than trying to be someone else.

Your answer should include
- a new title
- at least 3 details from the tale to support your title

You may have a couple of ideas for a title. Choose a title that is creative and accurate. Be sure you can support it with details in the tale.

Examples of titles:

"The Monkey"—This title is incomplete because the tale is about more than the monkey.

"Lunchtime"—This title identifies the setting, but the tale is about much more.

"The Monkey and the Rabbit"—This title is accurate, but not very creative.

"Act Natural"—This title is accurate and creative, but is too much like the original title.

"Appreciate Being Different" and "Jungle Lessons" are both better titles because they are accurate and creative.

31. This African folktale teaches a lesson. Which lesson does the folktale teach best? Use details from the tale to support your answer.

■ Love your neighbors for who they are.
■ Be yourself: don't try to be something you're not.

Sample Response

There is an important lesson to be learned in the African folk-tale, "Doing What Comes Naturally." The lesson is, "Be yourself: don't try to be something you're not." The monkey scratches and the rabbit looks around, naturally. Each of them tries to stop these behaviors to be more like the other and to please the other. The rabbit and the monkey realize how difficult it is to change. They both decide that it is better to simply be themselves.

Your answer should include:
■ identification of the tale—use the title
■ one of the lessons given
■ details from the tale to support the lesson
■ details to make your story interesting to the reader

32. Use Aunt Tillie's web site to complete the boxes below. Your answer must include

■ one fact about mountains in Alaska
■ one fact about the Alaskan flag
■ one fact about Alaskan state symbols

Include facts from the web site only.

Sample Response

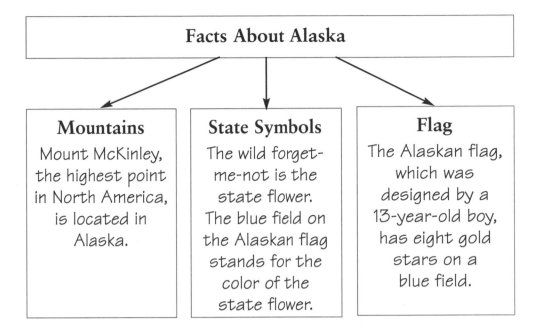

Facts About Alaska

Mountains	State Symbols	Flag
Mount McKinley, the highest point in North America, is located in Alaska.	The wild forget-me-not is the state flower. The blue field on the Alaskan flag stands for the color of the state flower.	The Alaskan flag, which was designed by a 13-year-old boy, has eight gold stars on a blue field.

THERE ARE OTHER POSSIBLE ANSWERS.

Note: All answers must be based on information from the web site. They must be written in the correct box. For example, a correct fact about the Alaskan flag would be considered wrong if it is written in the box labeled "Mountains."

All answers must be based on "facts" given in the web site, rather than opinions. A response "I like the Alaskan flag" or "The Alaskan flag is pretty" is not correct because it is an opinion, not a fact.

33. Use information from the e-mail to complete the web with dogmushing facts.

Sample Response

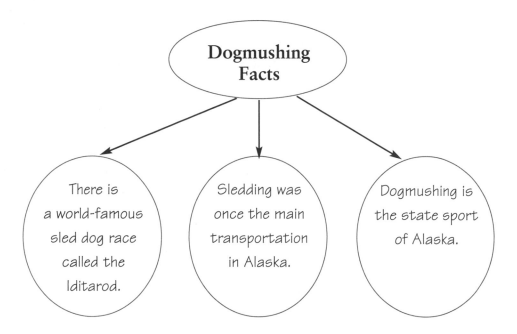

Dogmushing Facts

There is a world-famous sled dog race called the Iditarod.

Sledding was once the main transportation in Alaska.

Dogmushing is the state sport of Alaska.

Other acceptable answers to complete the chart above:

- Alaskans participate in many outdoor activities, including dogmushing.
- Iditarod is a famous sled dog race from Anchorage to Nome.
- The Iditarod is a well-known sled dog race, which lasts for about nine days.
- Dogmushers and their faithful, strong dogs race along icy tundra in the Iditarod.

34. Write an e-mail in response to the e-mail sent by the fourth-grade students in Alaska. In your e-mail, be sure to

- include at least 3 interesting details about New York State
- ask questions about the information presented by the Alaskan students in their e-mail, so that you can learn more about life in Alaska

Sample Response

To: Fourth-Grade Students in Alaska
From: Fourth-Grade Students in New York State

Re: Eager to be e-pals

Hello e-pals from the Land of the Midnight Sun,

Thank you for your e-mail, which had many interesting facts about Alaska. My classmates and I would also like to become e-pals with students in another state.

Like Alaskans, New Yorkers enjoy longer days in the summer, but they are only a few hours longer than winter days. I think it would be wonderful to have sunshine until almost 11:00 P.M. My friends and I like to ride our bikes and play soccer in the summer. During the winter, we go sledding and skating. What kind of indoor activities do you like to do?

Dogmushing seems like an exciting sport. Have you ever tried it? Popular sports in New York are hockey, football, and baseball. We do not have a state sport.

Please e-mail me again soon.

Your New Friend from the Empire State

---

35. Your teacher has encouraged your class to become e-pals with students from another state. You have received many e-mails from around the country. You have decided that you would like to correspond with students in Alaska. It is your job to write a speech to present to your classmates to convince them to vote for writing to Alaskan e-pals. Be sure to use information from the web site and the e-mail.

Sample Response

There are many reasons that we should be e-pals with the class from Alaska.

By choosing Alaskan e-pals, our class would learn interesting information about a place that is both different from, but also similar to, our own state. Did you know that Alaskans do not live in igloos and that the average yearly snowfall in Alaska is 69 inches? That amount of snowfall is less than some parts of New York State might receive in an average year.

Alaskans know how to have fun and enjoy life. They enjoy doing many exciting outdoor activities, such as canoeing, biking, and rock climbing. Wouldn't it be exciting to share information with them about those adventurous sports? We can also learn more about their world-famous sled dog race known as the Iditarod.

Here are a couple of fascinating facts about Alaska. During the summer, in some of the northernmost parts of the state, the sun does not set for 84 days. In other parts of Alaska, there is sunlight until almost 11:00 P.M. Now, we know why Alaska is sometimes called, "Land of the Midnight Sun."

Please join me and vote for Alaskan e-pals. You will <u>not</u> be disappointed, and you'll see why the name Alaska means "great land."

Chart your answers to be sure that you have facts from both selections. This can be done before writing, in the planning stage.

Facts from the Web Site	Facts from the e-mail
"great land" snowfall per year	Land of the Midnight Sun dogmushing hours of sunlight canoeing, biking, and rock climbing

PRACTICE TEST 2

"Dandelion"

1. **C** In the beginning of the poem, the dandelion is described as having fluffy hair. When a dandelion is fully seeded, its seeds are attached to stems with white fluffy threads (hair).

2. **F** In the beginning of the poem, the dandelion is described as being pretty and having lovely hair. However, the poem ends sadly ("sad to tell") with her hair blowing away.

3. **D** The poem states that the dandelion's hair *blew* many miles away. A gust of wind would cause things such as her hair to blow away.

4. **H** The poem mentions sunshine and "summer air."

5. **A** The poet is "sad to tell" that the dandelion's charming hair blew away. The poet then must have liked her hair or found it "pleasing."

"How to Weigh an Elephant"

6. **H** The boy is clever; his creative idea worked. The other answer choices are not supported by information from the tale.

7. **B** According to the tale, after the emperor had received the elephant, he was amazed by its size. He then wanted to know the weight of the animal.

8. **J** When the emperor received the elephant, he was amazed by the size of the creature. The word "creature" then refers to the elephant.

9. **B** The emperor knows that the young boy was the one who had determined the elephant's weight. He will then most likely ask the boy for help if he has future problems to be solved.

10. **H** The boy's creative idea solved the emperor's problem. Choice **F** is not correct because younger people are not *always* smarter than older people. There is no proof in the tale to support the remaining choices, **G** and **J**.

11. **B** The emperor commanded his advisors to solve his problem. A word to describe him would then be "demanding." The other choices (kind, clever, helpful) would not make sense.

12. **J** The emperor was amazed at the size of the elephant; it was too big for normal-sized scales.

13. **B** The advisors were not able to weigh the elephant. Choice **A** happened right after the emperor had received the gift. Choices **C** and **D** happened after it was discovered that the young boy's idea had worked.

"Cobwebs"

14. **F** The cobwebs were lying on grasses and shining in the sun, so they would most likely be found in a field.

15. **C** The cobwebs are referred to as "fairy lace-work."

16. **J** The "you" in the poem refers to the cobwebs.

17. **D** "Lace-work" describes the "O so finely spun" cobwebs.

18. **H** The poet's choice of language in the poem shows a love for cobwebs: "Dainty fairy lace-work, O so finely spun."

19. **A** According to the information given, dainty and delicate are synonyms (dainty = delicate). The opposite (antonym) of dainty is strong.

"The Original Potato Chip"

20. **J** The article was written to inform readers about the accidental invention of potato chips. It does not teach readers how to make potato chips (choice **F**), nor does it persuade us to eat chips (choice **G**). Choice **H** is also incorrect because the article does not explore the different types of potato chips (barbecue, sour cream and onion, etc.).

21. **D** The word mister was <u>not</u> used to identify the visitor. All other word choices were used.

22. **G** Potato chips were first served in Saratoga, New York. French fries were first served in Paris, France.

23. **A** The customer sent the French fries back to the kitchen because they were too thick.

24. **J** A customer had made the chef angry, so the chef made the potato chips to get back at the customer.

"The Rain"

25. **C** According to the first few lines in the poem, the rain wants the people inside the house to open the window and let it in.

26. **J** The rain bounced on the step and the sidewalk, which made people run.

27. **B** *Dash* means rush. Substitute each letter choice into the sentence, "The windows are shut or I'd dash right in." The word choices "tap" and "shut" would not

make sense in the sentence. The poet uses strong words to describe what the merry rain wants to do. The rain wants to splash down on the carpet and stream down the attic stairs. So, the rain would most likely want to rush (a strong word) right in, rather than just "step" in.

28. **G** The rain has been tapping outside, but it has not been able to do what it wants to do (splash on the carpet, splash in the window, and stream down the attic stairs).

29. Complete the boxes below with Crocodile's character traits from the tale.

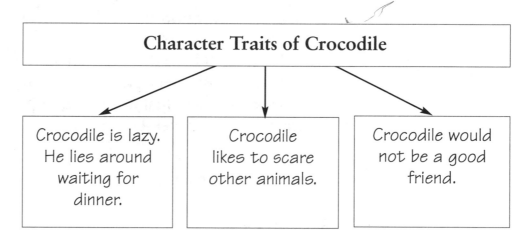

Other acceptable answers:

Crocodile is mean.
He has no manners.
He is not trustworthy.
Crocodile thinks only of himself.
He will snap at you when given a chance.

30. In the tale "How the Ostrich Got His Long Neck," the statement "Elephant also added his own two cents" means

Elephant was very worried about Ostrich wanting to be friends with Crocodile. He "added his own two cents," meaning he gave his advice to stay away from the crocodile. He said that Crocodile thinks only of himself and will snap at others when given a chance.

Tips for understanding quotations:
■ Review your notes for any information that may help explain the quotation.
■ Name the character(s) involved.
■ Restate the quotation using different words.

31. In the tale "How the Ostrich Got His Long Neck," Ostrich learns a very good lesson. Which lesson below does the tale best teach? Use examples from the tale to support your choice.

■ Listen to your friend's advice.
■ Choosing the wrong friends can be bad for you.

Sample Response

In the tale "How the Ostrich Got His Long Neck," Ostrich learns that it is wise to listen to his friends' advice. Because he ignored his friends' warnings about Crocodile, Ostrich finds himself in great danger.

Monkey, Wildebeest, and Elephant agreed that their animal buddy, Ostrich, should stay away from Crocodile. They described Crocodile as a mean, lazy, selfish animal who would not be a true pal. As Elephant had commented to Ostrich, Crocodile "will snap at you if he gets a chance."

Ostrich did not follow his friends' warnings and decided to play with Crocodile one dreary day. Crocodile almost ended up biting Ostrich's head off.

Ostrich has a very long neck, today, because he had to keep pulling his head out of Crocodile's jaws. His stretched neck is a constant reminder to him that he should listen to his friends' advice.

32. According to the newsletter, what are some of the positive and negative effects technology may have on the lives of children?

Positive Effects of Technology on Lives of Children	Negative Effects of Technology on Lives of Children
Children can meet and get to know other children from faraway places.	Children can have neck injuries from sitting at the computer with poor posture, for long periods of time.
Children can have chats with experts to get information.	Sometimes children may not be safe; e-mail should be monitored.

Other Positive Effects (+)	Other Negative Effects (−)
Children enjoy playing video games. Communication is improved; different languages can be translated. Children can join cooperative projects.	Back injuries Wrist injuries Some games may be violent

33. What are "wearable computers"? What are some reasons people might be excited about these new inventions? Be sure to use examples from the article.

Sample Response

Wearable computers are clothes with computers built into them. Some wearable computers will be used for entertainment purposes, such as a hooded jacket that plays music. Others are designed to improve safety, like the clothes for soldiers that will warn them of approaching danger. Doctors are experimenting with projection glasses, which would help them during surgery. Wearable computers will someday be used for many exciting purposes, and they may make our lives better and more interesting.

Note the 3 examples from the article.

34. According to the article, why are we not able to buy all of these inventions in the stores today?

Sample Response

Many of the wearable computer inventions are not in the stores yet. Some models are being tested, like the computers in sneakers that tell how fast a runner is moving and the projection glasses for doctors doing surgery.

The wearable computers need a fabric that will last over time. Presently, the fabric holding the technology is not strong enough, but new fabrics are being tested. When such problems are solved, the wearable computer inventions will be sold to the public.

Note the 3 examples from the article.

35. Technology is everywhere today. It affects almost every part of our life. What are some of the ways that technology influences lives?

Be sure to include examples from both the newsletter and the article.

Sample Response

Technology is a major part of our world today. It affects almost every area of our lives.

Technology influences our military and doctors. Computer experts are working together with makers of clothing to help protect our soldiers. Their goal is to invent a "wearable computer" that would warn soldiers of approaching vehicles. Some doctors are experimenting with projection glasses, which would help them during surgery.

Children use the computer for many reasons. They enjoy playing video games and e-mailing friends in faraway places. Technology is also making it easier for children and adults to find and learn information.

Technology affects our safety, health, pleasure time, and learning. Each year, new inventions make the influence of technology in our lives even greater.

Did you use examples from both reading selections?

Information from Newsletter Technology	Information from Article
Kids play video games. Kids make long-distance friends.	Soldiers use technology. Doctors use technology. New inventions are coming.

PRACTICE TEST 3

"The Wind and the Sun"

1. **D** This is the only answer supported by the story. "The North Wind bragged of great strength," and "bragged" is a synonym for the word "boasted." The wind blew hard and made the man shiver, eliminating answers A, B, and C.

2. **G** The first thing that happened "right after" the wind started blowing was the birds clinging to the trees, A happened before the wind blew, C and D happened after, but not right after.

3. **D** This is the contest proposed by the Sun. A, B, C all happened but were not part of winning the contest.

4. **F** The Wind asks the question of the Sun, "How did you do that?" and "that" refers to the man taking his coat off.

5. **C** The lesson of the tale is that gentleness can be strong.

6. **H** The word "protested" means "argued"; the sentence is about the disagreement.

"The Barn Spider"

7. **A** This is an informational article about spiders and not about spider characters.

8. **H** This information is in the article in paragraph 1.

9. **D** A, B, and C are all incorrect. D is stated in the article.

10. **G** This is a vocabulary question. Clues to the meaning of the word "worn" are found later in the paragraph: "If the web is not heavily damaged from the nighttime catches...."

11. D This information is stated in the article at the beginning of paragraph 2.

12. G This information is stated in the article in paragraph 2.

"The History of the Piggy Bank"

13. D This is the only choice that fits between the other two events. A and C would be after the last event listed; B would have been before the first listed choice.

14. H This information is in paragraph 2. All three other choices are in the article but are not a reference to the quote. Always look back in the article for the quote and look for sentences around the quote for clues.

15. A This is the best choice. B, C, and D are incorrect statements.

16. F This information is in the first paragraph.

17. B This is the best answer to the question.

"Can Animals Predict the Weather?"

18. H This information is stated in paragraph 4.

19. A Choices B, C, and D are all true statements about animals predicting rain. The information can be found in paragraph 3.

20. H The word "harsh" is a synonym for the word "severe."

21. D This is the correct answer. "Before" is the key word in the question.

22. F This answer is stated in paragraph 5 of the article.

"An American Symbol"

23. **C** Once endangered … , the population continues to gain; means the Bald Eagle is no longer endangered.

24. **J** America was the new land in 1782.

25. **B** Ben Franklin thought "the Eagle's character was lacking," that it did not have good character. The other answers are not supported by the poem.

26. **F** The poem also mentions "another native bird, the turkey."

27. **C** All the choices are direct quotes from the poem; images are renowned or famous pictures.

28. **J** The only answer stated in the poem is "has good eyesight."

"The Whistling Champ"

29. Complete the boxes below to describe Emily's change of feelings.

Parts of the Story	Feelings About the Trophy
Beginning of the story	The trophy stood tall and proud on her grandfather's shelf. Emily felt the trophy was mocking her. She was embarrassed that she could not whistle.
End of the story	The trophy was now on Emily's book shelf, a gift from her grandfather. She happily whistled herself to sleep, she was proud of herself.

30. Why do you think Emily's grandfather gave her the championship trophy at the end of the story? Use examples from the story to support your answer.

Sample Response

Emily's grandfather knew that Emily worked very hard to learn to whistle. She wanted a lesson everytime she visited. She practiced every chance she had, during her chores, walking to the bus stop. She did not give up. Her grandfather was proud that she learned to whistle, but he was even prouder that she didn't give up. After all, that was the greatest lesson of all. She was the hardest working whistler.

31. How did Emily's feelings change from beginning to the end of the story? What causes the change? Use details from the story to support your answer.

- include how Emily feels at the beginning of the story
- describe how Emily feels at the end of the story
- explain what causes the changes in her feelings.
- use examples from the story to support your answer

Sample Response

Emily feels very discouraged by her inablity to whistle. She tries and tries and she can not whistle. Her whole family can whistle, even her little brother. She keeps trying to learn to whistle, day after day. Then one day after a lot of practice she is able to whistle a few notes. She can't wait to tell her grandfather, after all he is a whistling champ. She knows he will be proud of her. When she whistles for her grandfather he gives her his championship trophy. He tells her it is because she is the hardest working whistler. He is proud of her for trying so hard and she is proud of herself. She worked very hard and was finally able to whistle.

32. Complete the chart below with the three details from the story to explain the unique homing abilities of pigeons.

Reasons for the Homing Ability of Pigeons
(1) Pigeons can tell north, south, east, and west by using the sun.
(2) Pigeons have a tiny bit of magnetite in their heads. It is like having a tiny compass in their heads.
(3) Pigeons are able to smell home. The can smell home in the blowing wind.

33. Why were pigeons used to help people communicate? How did that method of communication change over time?

Sample Response

Pigeons were used to communicate between people in faraway places. They were sent with messages that would take riders on horseback weeks to deliver. They delivered news throughout the world. Today they are used to race and compete with. A doctor in France uses them to carry blood to the lab. Racing pigeons are used in competitions.

34. Why were smoke signals used to help people communicate? How did that method of communication change over time?

Sample Response

Smoke signals were used to communicate between people over long distances. Native Americans used them as signals. The Chinese also used them. Codes of smoke were used to send messages. Today smoke signals are used by Boy Scouts to signal information when other forms of communication are not available.

35. How were the carrier pigeons and smoke signal methods of communications alike? How are they different? How have both methods changed?

■ tell how the smoke signals and carrier pigeons are alike
■ tell how smoke signals and carrier pigeons are different
■ tell how both methods of communication change
■ use details from both stories to support your answer
■ check your writing for correct spellings, grammar, capitalization, and punctuation

Sample Response

Smoke signals and homing pigeons are similar because long ago they helped people communicate over long distances. They were both unpredictable because pigeons got lost and smoke signals were influenced by the weather. They were different because smoke signals were seen by many and codes needed to be set so that the communication could be a secret.

Today smoke signals are used in times of emergency, and the codes are understood by all. Homing pigeons are used today in competitions. People race pigeons for speed and accuracy of flight.

INDEX